10 DAYS THAT CHANGED AMERICA

VOLUME 1: THE COLONIAL YEARS

About the Authors

Terry D. Bilhartz is a professor of history at Sam Houston State University who has taught about 18,000 students during his career. He is the author of more than 50 articles and book chapters in the fields of history, religion, philosophy, psychology, and medicine, and has written scripts for public television documentaries. He is the author of *Urban Religion and the Second Great Awakening*, *Francis Asbury's America*, *Images of Texas in the Nation* (with Paul Ruffin), *Constructing the American Past* (with Elliot Gorn and Randy Roberts), *Sacred Words: A Source Book on the Great Religions of the World*, and *Currents in American History* (with Alan Elliott). Bilhartz holds degrees from Dallas Baptist College (BS), Emory University (MA), and the George Washington University (PhD), and has completed post-doctoral studies in history and religion at Vanderbilt University, Stanford University, the University of Connecticut, the East-West Center at the University of Hawaii, and the Australian National University.

Alan C. Elliott is the Director of Statistical Consulting in the Department of Statistical Science at Southern Methodist University. He is the author of numerous academic articles and over 30 books on topics including science, history, and biography. Current books include *A Daily Dose of the American Dream*; *Texas Ingenuity: Inventions, Inventors & Innovators*; *Legendary Locals of Oak Cliff*; *Images of America: Oak Cliff*; and *Currents in American History* (with Terry Bilhartz.) Technical books include *SAS Essentials*, *Statistical Analysis Quick Reference Guidebook*, and *Applied Time Series Analysis*. He specializes in writing techniques designed to make challenging subjects easy to understand.

10 DAYS THAT CHANGED AMERICA

Volume 1: The Colonial Years

Terry D. Bilhartz and Alan C. Elliott

2014
GREEN PUBLISHING HOUSE. LLC
College Station, Texas

10 Days That Changed America, Volume 1: The Colonial Years

Copyright © 2014 by Green Publishing House, LLC

All rights reserved. Printed in the United States of America. No part of this book may be reproduced or distributed in any form or by any means, or stored in a database or retrieval system, without written permission from the publisher, Green Publishing House, LLD, including, but limited to, in any network or other electronic storage or transmission, or broadcast for distance learning.

Some ancillaries, including electronic and print components, may not be available to customers outside of the United States.

ISBN 978-1-63432-000-9 (paperback)
ISBN 978-1-63432-001-6 (ePub)
ISBN 978-1-63432-002-3 (pdf)
ISBN 978-1-63432-003-0 (mobi)
ISBN 978-1-63432-004-7 (audio)

The Internet addresses listed in the text were accurate at the time of publication. The inclusion of a website does not indicate an endorsement by the authors or Green Publishing House, LLC, and Green Publishing House does not guarantee the accuracy of the information presented at these sites.

www.GreenPublishingHouse.com

To our parents and mentors who considered us their children

Skipper and Joy Bilhartz
Tom Samford and Ida Scirratt Elliott
Joseph and Carol Abston
Paul and Ann Morell

About Green Publishing House, LLC

Green Publishing House is a Limited Liability Corporation dedicated to the production and global distribution of scholarly, peer-reviewed, academic books and high quality general interest trade books. Green Publishing House partners with numerous distributors to deliver valued books across multiple platforms (digital and print) at competitive costs.

The central mission of Green Publishing House is to deliver high quality digital textbooks and trade books to readers at low prices. Going digital is not only environmentally responsible and less expensive to readers, but it also offers our clients the opportunity to receive up-to-date scholarly resources on a moment's notice from millions of locations worldwide.

Although the number of digital readers is growing every year, because everyone may not have access to the internet and eBook readers, and because some individuals, book reviewers, and libraries may prefer hard copy texts, the company also offers print copies of its books. To remain loyal to its central mission, however, the company encourages the purchase of digital versions of its books, and cheerfully donates a portion of the revenue it receives from its print copy sales to educational and charitable institutions.

Detailed Table of Contents

Preface	1

Chapter 1:
History and Historians:
Making Sense of the Full Catastrophe of Life

A Concise Guide for Training Historians	7
What is History?	9
Envisioning a Time Before History	14
The Genesis of History	17
The Methods of History	21
Understanding Historical Questions & the Limits of History	24
It's About Time: The Agony & Ecstasy of Dating	29
It's About Integrity: The Ethics of Creating History	33
The Purpose and Structure of *10 Days*	35
Historians at Work: How to Use this Text	41
Probing the Sources: From Story to History	41
Document 1: Excerpts from Genesis (*KJV*)	42
Document 2: Excerpts from Herodotus, *The Histories*	43
What Others Say: Investigating Competing Historical Arguments	44
Document 1: Selected Quotes – Historians on History	46
Looking Backward/Looking Forward: Thinking Historically	49
Suggested Readings	50
Online Resources	51
A Premise and a Challenge	51

Chapter 2:
An Uneven Exchange, October 12, 1492:
Christopher Columbus and the
Consequences of Contact

PRELUDE	55
America Before Columbus	58
Historians & the First Inhabitants of America	59
Agricultural Transformation & Its Consequences	63
The Diverse Cultures of North America	66
Europe Before Columbus	70
Christendom at Age 1000	71
Temperatures, Food and Disease	72
Rise of Trade, Towns and Technology	75
THE BIG EVENT	
Columbus and His Vision	79
Columbus Sailed the Ocean Blue, But Why 1492?	82
Contact in the Eyes of Columbus & the Tainos	85
POSTLUDE	
Political & Economic Consequences of Contact	86
The Demographic Impacts of Contact	91
Environmental & Cultural Consequences of Contact	94
PROBING THE SOURCES: Words from the Spanish Monarchs & Columbus	96
Document 1: Privileges and Prerogatives Granted by Their Catholic Majesties (1492)	97
Document 2: Excerpts from the Journal of Columbus's First Voyage	99
WHAT OTHERS SAY: Remembering Christopher Columbus	102
Document 1: Excerpts from Washington Irving, *A History of the Life and Voyages of Christopher Columbus* (1828)	104

Document 2: Excerpts from Herbert Baxter Adams,
 Columbus and His Discovery of America
 (Johns Hopkins Press, 1892)   108
Document 3: Excerpts from David E. Stannard,
 American Holocaust (Oxford University
 Press, 1992)   113
LOOKING BACKWARD/LOOKING FORWARD:
 Exploring the Consequences of Contact   115
SUGGESTED READINGS   116
ONLINE RESOURCES   117

Chapter 3:
Divorcing Church and State, October 9, 1635: John Winthrop and the Banishment of Roger Williams

PRELUDE   121
 After Columbus: A Century of Exploration
  & Reformation   123
 The English Reformation: The Religion of
  Henry VIII & His Children   129
 God, Gold and the Colonization of
  North America   133
 Early American Migrants: Gentlemen,
  Servants & Slaves   139
THE BIG EVENT
 Puritans, Pilgrims & the Settlement of
  New England   151
 Reform or Perish: Religious Crisis & the
  Settlement of Massachusetts Bay   155
 Troubles in Zion: The Case of Roger Williams   162
POSTLUDE
 Diversifying the New England Way   166
 Indian Conflicts & the Reexamination
  of the Puritan Mission   171
 The World Outside of New England   175

PROBING THE SOURCES: Competing Visions –
    Words from Winthrop & Williams   181
  Document 1: Excerpts from John Winthrop,
    "A Model of Christian Charity" (1630)   182
  Document 2: Excerpts from Roger Williams,
    The Bloudy Tenet of Persecution (1644)   186
WHAT OTHERS SAY: Historians on the Legacy of
    Winthrop & Williams   189
  Document 1: Excerpts from Perry Miller,
    *Roger Williams: His Contributions to the
    American Tradition* (Bobbs-Merrill, 1953)   189
  Document 2: Excerpts from Edmund Morgan,
    *The Puritan Dilemma: The Story of John
    Winthrop* (Harper Collins, 1958)   191
  Document 3: Excerpts from John M. Barry,
    *Roger Williams and the Creation of the
    American Soul: Church, State, and the
    Birth of Liberty* (Viking, 2012)   193
LOOKING BACKWARD/LOOKING FORWARD:
    Viewing Themes Across Time and Place   195
SUGGESTED READINGS   196
ONLINE RESOURCES   197

Chapter 4:
Awakening the Enlightened, November 8, 1739: George Whitefield, Benjamin Franklin and the Wars & Cultural Wars of the 18th Century

PRELUDE   201
  Clashing Empires: A Glorious Revolution &
    4 World Wars   203
  America in Transition: Saints to Sellers,
    Servants to Slaves   212
  The Facts of Life: Migration, Sex and Marriage   220
THE BIG EVENT
  A Brewing Cultural War: Enlightenment
    & Awakenings   226

An Odd Couple Meet: Ben Franklin & George
    Whitefield in Philadelphia   231
The Afterglow: Religious Affairs After
    Whitefield   236
POSTLUDE
    Immediate Consequences: Society & Culture
        at Mid-Century   238
    Enduring Consequences: Giving Birth to the
        American Mind   243
PROBING THE SOURCES: The Awakening
    Among Friends and Foes   249
    Document 1: Excerpts from *The Memoirs of*
        Benjamin Franklin (1784)   250
    Document 2: Excerpts from Gilbert Tennent,
        Danger of an Unconverted Minister (1740)   259
    Document 3: Excerpts from Charles Chauncy,
        Enthusiasm Described and Caution'd
        Against (1742)   261
WHAT OTHERS SAY: The Awakening and Its
    Consequences   265
    Document 1: Excerpts from Jon Butler, *Awash*
        in a Sea of Faith: Christianizing the American
        People (Harvard University Press, 1990)   265
    Document 2: Excerpts from Thomas S. Kidd,
        God of Liberty: A Religious History of the
        American Revolution (Basic Books, 2010)   267
    Document 3: Excerpts from Frank Lambert,
        Inventing the "Great Awakening" (Princeton
        University Press, 1999)   269
LOOKING BACKWARD/LOOKING FORWARD:
    Assigning Cause & Assessing Effect   271
SUGGESTED READINGS   272
ONLINE RESOURCES   274

INDEX   277

Preface

Sitting on my desk are three beautiful new editions of college history survey textbooks. I did not request these copies, but the publishers sent them to me to encourage me to adopt them in my classes. If I were to ask my one- and four-year-old grandsons, Carson and Peyton, to peruse these books and say a word that described them, I suspect the word that would come to their minds would be "heavy." If I were to ask my six-year-old grandson, Preston, the same question, he might add the descriptive word "colorful." These descriptions, "heavy" and "colorful," would be accurate because the average weight of these is about forty ounces, and multi-colors exist on almost every page. If I then were to ask college freshmen in a university book store to comment on these textbooks, I suspect their most common answer would be "expensive." This also would be an appropriate answer because the average 2014 price tags for these texts is about $130, an expensive investment for most college freshmen, even if this still is a lower price than textbooks in many other disciplines.

For me, an instructor who wants to instill my passion for history into the unfortunate students who don't want to take this course, but must do so in order to satisfy a degree requirement for their major, the words that I would use to describe these texts would be "comprehensive but scattered."

I say this because it seems to me that these works aspire to be magazine look-alike books that say something about every topic of interest to contemporary academic historians. In order to cover the whole waterfront of the American past in an aesthetically pleasing fashion, virtually every page of these texts supplements the historical narrative with etchings (i.e., modern drawings meant to look like historic artifacts), highlighted boxes containing timelines, isolated quotes, short biographies or an assortment of other interesting but disjointed historical tidbits, and maps, portraits, and illustrations that easily can be accessed and expanded to a more useful size with a simple internet search.

In some texts, these supplemental features fill about one-half of the space allotted to each chapter. Valuable content is contained in these supplemental features, but according to adult learning theory, this content would more likely be delivered and retained if students played a more active role in constructing this content for themselves rather than simply having it presented to them in disjointed segments.

I am not opposed to the creation of artfully designed, full-color, comprehensive, and expensive textbooks that also can duplicate as attractive coffee table books to adorn home libraries and living rooms. In fact, I have been the author of such textbooks with some of the same publishing houses.

However, after spending several decades in the classroom experimenting with ways to make the past come alive to students – many of whom arrive with little initial interest in history – and for part of that time serving simultaneously as a college administrator concerned with the rising price of textbooks, I no longer embrace a "more is better" educational philosophy.

My years of experience teach me that streamlined, pedagogically focused, and environmentally and consumer friendly textbooks offer more economic and educational value to students than beautiful, heavy, and expensive comprehensive textbooks.

10 Days That Changed America intertwines with its narrative primary sources, historiographical essays, and problem-based learning exercises. Yet these features are not mere add-ons, but are essential to the design of each chapter. The purpose of this textbook is not only to present a narrative of the past in a lively and readable style that can be digested and remembered by its readers, but it also is to train students how to do the work of historians. Every page of the volume is designed with this end.

Although Green Publishing House also offers hard copy versions of this textbook, *10 Days That Changed*

America was written to be read on an eBook reader. Therefore, it uses shorter paragraphs and makes greater use of abbreviations in headings than is standard protocol for hardcover books. Pieces of this text were originally published in a more standard textbook format as *Currents in American History* (ME Sharpe, 2007).

The authors of this text would like to extend their thanks to a network of friends and colleagues who have helped to make this work possible. Special thanks goes to professors Rosanne Barker, Ty Cashion, Caroline Crimm, Yvonne Frear, Katherine Gaskamp, Jeff Littlejohn, James Olson, Darren Pierson, Bernadette Pruitt, Blake Tritico, and Susannah Ural for not only reviewing early drafts, but also on occasions piloting portions of the text with some of their students. We also thank Rocky Bilhartz, Lindsey Bilhartz, Patty Bilhartz, Bob and Carol Bogart, Steve Drummond, Mary Elliott, William Elliott, Betty Gore, Kyle Longley, Scott Maxwell, Teri Maxwell, Bryant Simon, LenPaul Stadler, Michael L. Tate, and Wayne Woodward who assisted us as proofreaders and friendly critics. We also thank the academic historians initially known to us only by their insightful comments who reviewed early drafts of this work.

Finally, to the students who will be asked by their teachers to read this text, the authors of this textbook would like to send you a challenge. At the end of the semester, no matter what opinions you hold, we encourage you to send to the Green Publishing House website your thoughts about history in general and about this textbook in particular. Did reading this text change your attitude about history? Did it help you to become a better historian? Specifically, what pieces of the text did you find to be most and least helpful? What changes would you recommend in future editions?

      The insights you provide will be helpful to both future students and to the authors of this text. And for those who offer constructive criticism, do not be surprised if the next edition of this textbook incorporates some of your ideas.

From the desk of

Terry D. Bilhartz
Professor of History
Sam Houston State University
July 2014

Chapter 1:
History and Historians:
Making Sense of the Full Catastrophe of Life

A Concise Guide for Training Historians

Hundreds of graduating seniors surrounded by two thousand supporting guests crammed into a university coliseum for a spring graduation. The speaker on this occasion was a distinguished physician who grew up in San Antonio, Texas, the son of hardworking Mexican immigrants. As a young man he was a gifted athlete, earning All-American honors as a receiver on his college's football team. After a brief stint in the NFL, he pursued a career in medicine, gaining international recognition as an expert in the field of sports-related facial injuries.

He opened his address by telling the graduates that each of them would leave the building with something that no one else would have. This gift was not a diploma, for thousands of others on that day would receive this honor. Instead, the unique gift that was given to each graduate was the privilege of being in charge of his or her own destiny. The speaker followed with standard platitudes fitted to this occasion, telling the graduates to shoot for the stars, to work hard to reach their dreams, to learn from mentors who would assist them along the way, and to remember as their guide Booker T. Washington's definition of achievement: "Success is to be measured not so much by the position that one has reached in life as by the obstacles which one has overcome."

While the speaker's words were well-articulated, what made the address so powerful was the way he illustrated each point with stories from his own life. To illustrate his final point, for example, he spoke about an incident that occurred during his medical residency when he traveled to a remote region of Brazil to perform facial reconstruction surgeries on the indigenous population. Unfortunately, on this occasion an infant child who underwent a cleft lip repair perished on his operating table. Frustrated at the loss of his first patient, the surgeon tore off his surgical gloves and started to leave the makeshift jungle clinic when his mentor ordered him to return to the table, finish the surgical repair, and carry the deceased child back to his parents.

With a somber tone, the speaker recounted his memory of the parents' reaction to the tragic news. Although deeply saddened, the parents found some comfort in gazing at the face of their baby because, as was the custom in their village, they believed that while God would never accept a blemished child into paradise, they felt that their now beautiful baby had been transported to heaven.

Only moments after the speaker finished his remarks, someone in the coliseum audience slumped in his seat. Seeing the distress of the subject from the podium, the physician speaker swiftly left the stage to attend to the medical needs of the stricken man. As people in the crowd strained their necks to get a glimpse of what was happening, a hush filled the coliseum, until someone looking down from the upper tier broke the silence by shouting out to one of the graduates below. This outburst triggered another shout from the bleachers. Although the Master-of-Ceremonies on the podium asked the crowd to be patient while the stricken man was receiving care, this request for decorum had little effect, as growing numbers in the audience used the pause in the ceremonies to dance and wave and shout words of celebration to the cap-and-gown-dressed graduates below. The catcalls quieted only when uniformed officers placed themselves more visibly in the aisles of the coliseum. Meanwhile, one faculty member experiencing the moment remarked to himself: "The human race, is all over the place."

WHAT IS HISTORY?

If a historian were asked to research and produce an interpretive account of this commencement exercise, what type of research would the historian conduct, and what would the outline of the finished history product look like? Perhaps the most accurate answer to this question would be the simple response: there are multiple valid answers to this question.

To illustrate, most historians tasked with this assignment would be quick to gather additional evidence by locating any extant recordings of the event, by securing the commencement program with its lists of graduating students, and by conducting oral interviews with the graduating students and their friends and family who attended the event. The type of information scholars would glean from these new sources, however, as well as the types of secondary sources they would consult to provide context and significance to the event, would likely vary according to the interests, perspectives, and historical training of each historian.

A biographer, for instance, might be fascinated with the life details of the commencement speaker, and how his recipe for success and life experiences seemed to echo what others have referred to as "the American dream." A social historian might be more critical of the utility of the commencement speaker's advice, and contrast his biography with the lives of thousands of other children of Mexican immigrants whose lives did not follow the same trajectory as the speaker because of unmentioned and dissimilar social determinants. Another historian also might question the universality of the speaker's advice by noting that the ability to set goals and develop work and networking patterns to accomplish them is largely determined by chemical reactions at the cellular level, processes that are determined less by self-will than by inheritance, nutrition, and chance.

Still other historians might frame their histories around other details. A cultural historian with anthropological interests, for example, might choose to explore the rituals that were being practiced and violated during the commencement exercise, while a quantitative historian with sociological leanings might prefer to survey groups of people for their attitudes regarding the commencement speech and the commotion on the floor in an attempt to understand if these attitudes were influenced by age, gender, ethnicity, and economic class. Still others might seek to explore what the faculty observer meant when he reflected, "The human race, is all over the place."

In sum, if an account of a contemporaneous one-hour event taking place within a single building can produce such diverse histories, should we not expect to find that narratives of life in the past also will be complex stories of affairs that can be expressed in many different forms? This is not to suggest that there is no rubric that can be used to separate what constitutes compelling historical arguments from unpersuasive ones, but this does suggest that historians, perhaps more so than scholars trained in harder sciences, are generally comfortable acknowledging that there may be a variety of historically contingent routes to any particular event, and that meaningful insights can be gained from multiple investigative methodologies. Events of the past and records of these events may be concrete and unchanging, like the actual commencement ceremony and a video tape of it, but how historians record and explain these events is anything but uniform and static.

This work is based on these premises:

> *Historians exist, not to memorize and regurgitate the past, but to create "history."*

> *The primary objective of history survey courses is NOT to teach students everything they need to know about history, but to help them become historians.*

> *Historians of America understand that stories of the American past include complex and fascinating tales of intrigue, adventure, irony, and fulfilled and unfulfilled dreams that offer insight into why Americans think and behave as they do.*

If you do not fully agree with these assertions, you should realize that you are in good company because few students taking an introductory course in American history start the semester with this understanding. Actually, if you are skeptical of the truth of these statements, you have a disposition that would suit you well as a history student because historians are trained to become deliberative, creative thinkers not easily persuaded by authoritative claims, especially those presented without evidential support.

Thinking historically requires one to have the curiosity of a detective, and to maintain an open mind that seeks not so much to find agreement with but to understand foreign ideas, even if those ideas at face value sound absurd. As non-gullible, truth-seeking investigators, historians must strive to develop the skills that will enable them to view objects and ideas from multiple perspectives, and to understand how even arguments and behaviors that seem unintelligible to most conventional minds could be embraced by other peoples.

The authors of this book agree that the assertion that historians "create history" appears nonsensical for some critical thinkers who rightly insist that humans living at this moment do not possess the superpowers necessary to create the past. This point we concede, but our claim is not that historians create the actual past that was once experienced, but that historians create "history." In the following paragraphs we will attempt to clarify what we mean when we use the word "history." Understanding the distinction between what we call "history" and the actual past is central to understanding our central proposition that historians create history.

ENVISIONING A TIME BEFORE HISTORY

At various points in this text we will invite you to put down your eBook or book, or to hit the pause button on your audio-book reader device, in order to stop and reflect on a statement or a set of questions. Whenever you see the words "PAUSE-REFLECT-THINK" we encourage you to deliberate a moment on the idea before you.

In the next few moments, go on a mental journey by giving some thought to the following:

Envision a time before history. As you contemplate this idea, what images come to your mind? Moving forward, what prerequisites must exist for history to arise?

PAUSE-REFLECT-THINK

Most of us, when first asked to reflect on a time before history, create in our minds images of darkness, dinosaurs, or hairy Neanderthals. These images are accurate, but when thinking these thoughts, we probably are assuming that history means "the past" or, more specifically, "the human past." Although "the past" is indeed a definition of history, it is not the only definition. When students major in history, for instance, they do not major in "the past." Instead, they major in a subject or in a branch of knowledge known as "history."

Thus, "history," in this more technical sense, is not the past, but rather is a perception of the past that has been constructed by following a process that is often referred to as "the historical method." This method involves applying rules of evidence to sources (such as artifacts, letters on a page, audio recordings, physical visual images, etc.) that date to some distant time and place being studied. Historians (students of the past who practice this craft) call these distant sources "primary sources." The craft or method of history in its most basic form is an attempt to understand what life was like in the past by applying reasoned arguments to primary source materials.

History is not the only way to make sense of the past. Long before there were historians there were mythmakers who told stories of past times that explained how things came to be as they are. Recognizing this leads us to another set of questions:

When did people start trusting the historical method as the most reliable way to make sense of the past? In short, how old is history? Who invented it and why? And how has this approach to the past influenced the way modern Americans think and act?

These simple questions have complex answers that may surprise even serious students of history. Not yet even 2,500 years old, history as a discipline is not as old as many think. Neither is it universally recognized as the most credible way to explain life in the past. Indeed, even in the 21st century indigenous populations can be found on every continent that have no desire to use reasoned arguments drawn from primary sources to make sense of their past.

Yet, although a relatively new human invention, and one that still has not convinced all peoples of its value, the craft of history has had a profound impact on how peoples familiar with Western civilization, and more recently with Eastern civilization as well, think critically. In fact, the influence of history on how we organize our place in time is so engrained in our culture that many educated Americans find it difficult to approach the past in any other way.

To begin the search for the origins of history, at least for North Americans familiar with the advance of Western civilization, there is no better place to start than to investigate the ancient book that opens with the familiar line: "In the beginning God created the heavens and the earth."

THE GENESIS OF HISTORY

In this story from the book of Genesis, a work sacred to many that is contained in both the Hebrew and Christian Bibles, God speaks, creates, declares the creation to be good, and then calls it evening and morning, the end of day one. As the story continues, God speaks again, creating more than previously existed, declares the new creation to be good, and then calls it evening and morning, the end of day two. After more creations on days three, four, five, and six, God rests and declares the seventh day to be holy.

The Genesis story continues with a well-known account involving the characters Adam and Eve. This story and the subsequent Hebrew sacred stories make the point that human actions have consequences that can spoil the goodness of creation, but that obedience to the creator of life can bring blessings. To the ancient Hebrews, human decisions and actions were important and carried even sacred, ontological significance.

Although many other ancient peoples also had creation stories, the Genesis account has had the more profound influence on the development of Western Civilization. Genesis is important not because scholars consider it superior history or science (indeed, it was composed long before either of these disciplines was invented), but because it takes a novel approach to time and because it gives importance to the consequences of human activity.

Unlike the ancient Hebrews, other ancient peoples often passed down sacred stories that operated outside what moderns would call historic time and place. Many of the great stories of Greek mythology, for example, take place in the skies of Mount Olympus or at the bottom of the sea. In contrast, most of the activities in the Hebrew Bible take place at ground level, in a world that seems mostly recognizable to modern eyes.

More importantly, according to many ancients from both the East and the West, time did not flow forward as much as it moved in a circle like the spinning of a wheel. The sacred stories of many peoples from India to the Americas suggested that just as the sun followed its daily course and the moon followed its monthly rhythms, humans were born, matured, died, and then were returned back into a recycling cosmos. In cultures with sacred myths that viewed time as cyclic, there was less incentive to record daily activities or to fret about daily decisions. In an eternal cosmos with no beginning or end, but only transitions, the struggle to improve creation appeared to be an impossible and even unwanted ideal.

Unlike these contemporaries, however, the ancient Hebrews viewed time linearly and gave credence to the idea of progress. Time flowing forward from the past to the present in a straight line progression did not necessarily imply human progress, because regression also could occur, but it did at least suggest the possibility of improvement.

The sacred stories in the Hebrew Bible are principally theological compositions about the relationship between these people and their God. However, owing to the Hebrew construction of linear time and discussion of the cosmic events within earthly space, the ancient Hebrew narratives look more familiar to modern readers of history than many other ancient texts. The Hebrews did not invent the discipline we now call history, but their approach to time and place did lay the foundation for it.

History – that is, the intellectual discipline that uses reasoned evidence from extant sources to make sense of the past – owes its origins not to the Hebrews, but to the Greeks. The evolution of this discipline was slow. In the sixth century BCE, a few Greek thinkers became dissatisfied with the traditional mythological explanations for the creation of the cosmos from the activities of the gods. Trusting observation and reason over their sacred mysteries, these Greeks attempted to explain the natural world without making reference to the supernatural. With these investigations into the physical world, science, or at least a distant relative of it, was born.

About a century later, Herodotus, another Greek intellectual unconvinced by the explanations of the myths, determined to understand how society as he knew it came to be. Specifically, he wanted to understand the causes of the Greek-Persian War, the foremost event that framed the time in which he lived. Herodotus traveled to distant lands, looking for sources – some written, but mostly oral – that could help him find his answers. When his sources offered suggestions that defied observation and logic, he rejected them, demanding instead more reasonable explanations. Herodotus published his findings in a work entitled *The Histories,* a word that literally meant "inquiry" or "research." With this publication, Herodotus invented the genre of history.

Many readers today will not embrace the theology of the ancient Hebrews or the philosophies of the ancient Greeks, but most will accept the Hebraic arrangement of linear time and the Greek demand for causation arguments based on rational analysis of sources. This is because Western Civilization has been largely influenced by the ideas of the ancient Hebrews and Greeks. Like the precursors and creators of the discipline of history, most modern Americans view time as a continuous stream of forward moving, nonreversible events, with each event being both a product of previous actions and a force that influences the possibilities of future events. The present builds on the past, and every moment in time is shaped by it.

THE METHODS OF HISTORY

Since the time of Herodotus, critical thinkers whom we call historians have chosen to rely on the trustworthiness of linear time and on the necessity of using reason to unpack clues contained in primary sources as the most credible ways to understand the past and its relationship to the present. No universally accepted guidebook listing rules that historians must follow has been canonized. Historians, in short, do not embrace a single instruction book or bible that tells them how to make sense of the past.

Indeed, historians of different stripes and from different eras have disagreed and continue to disagree on a number of basic issues related to the purposes, scope, presentation and citation format, and methods of historical inquiry. Historians also have expressed and continue to express differing opinions regarding the objective versus the subjective nature of history, the constancy or cultural relativity of human nature, and whether history is better described as an art or a science. Exploring how and why historians disagree about both content and method is itself an intellectually stimulating field of study that historians have named "historiography." More will be said about this interesting field later in this volume.

Yet while historians disagree about many things, when asked to describe what they do and how they do it, most historians would share several common answers. One way to condense these common practices is to present them in a five step format that is compatible with the teaching style of instructors who embrace a project-based learning pedagogy.

These basic steps include:

(1) assimilate some knowledge about a segment of the past that has been suggested by critical thinkers who have carefully investigated the subject;

(2) create a probing question, the answers to which will build on or revise that conventionally accepted knowledge;

(3) compose a "need to know" list of background materials and sources from the era being studied that contains clues about the past relevant to the question at hand;

(4) extract and analyze information contained in these sources, expelling the irrelevant and less trustworthy information, and arranging the more pertinent information in some meaningful way that communicates a vision of the past; and

(5) construct a "history" by artfully publishing (which means "to circulate widely") an account of the past that can be comprehended by a targeted audience.

By reading this book with the eyes of a broad- and open-minded truth seeker; by releasing your imagination to create probing questions about the American past that excite your curiosity; by scavenging for primary sources that may offer clues to help you find answers to these questions; by extracting, analyzing, selecting, and organizing pertinent information obtained from these sources; and by artfully presenting your vision of the past to others, you not only will develop the skills of a historian, but you also will create history.

Be forewarned. No matter how long you practice this craft, you will never learn everything that is worth knowing about the past. The best that you can hope for is to become an expert in segments of the past, not the past in its entirety. The good news, however, is that most who begin a mental journey into the past will find the experience to be more rewarding than originally imagined. In fact, this book should come with a warning label: "creating history" can become addictive and change your life!

Before you start on this intellectual journey into the American past, it would be wise to be aware of some of the common pitfalls that often cause beginner historians to stumble. Here are some helpful hints to assist you on your journey into the past.

UNDERSTANDING HISTORICAL QUESTIONS & THE LIMITS OF HISTORY

To begin, you need to understand the scope and acknowledge the limitations of the historical method. While history is a powerful tool that can offer us insight into many things, it is not the only worthy branch of knowledge, and it cannot address all questions that are worthy of human interest.

Positioned on opposing sides of the discipline of history are two other ways to communicate truth: science and myth. Science, a discipline that gathers knowledge about the physical universe through observation and experimentation, aspires to discover general laws that can explain current natural phenomena and also, when the precise conditions are reproduced, to predict with accuracy future phenomena. The method of science is rigorous and its scope is limited to explorations of the material cosmos, not to the supernatural.

Myth also seeks to explain the origins of natural phenomena or aspects of human behavior, but unlike science, it is unfettered by method, and the scope of myth is limitless as there are no questions that it cannot seek to answer. The purpose of myth is to communicate the truth believed by a culture through the retelling of a traditional story.

In many ways history is located somewhere on a spectrum between science and myth. History is a branch of knowledge that is more concerned with unique, particular events than is science, and it therefore does not generally pronounce general laws that can predict future events. Like scientific truth, however, historical truth will not be accepted if its arguments are deemed to include "unreasonable" explanations.

Moreover, because the discipline of history is dependent on evidence contained in sources, historians cannot offer responses to questions for which there is no evidence. Although historians should aspire to find evidence to reconstruct all segments of the past, some past experiences may never be recovered. The past exists without sources, but without sources, there can be no history, at least by our definition of the word.

Sometimes uncertainties about the authenticity and/or the credibility of the sources rather than the lack of sources cloud our vision of the past. Because primary sources are historians' links to the past, when these links are broken by source authenticity or credibility questions, the historians' arguments, no matter how artfully presented, will not be compelling.

Determining the authenticity of the source – that is, who produced the source and when – is necessary to ensure that the source truly is what it purports to be and not a forgery or garbled reproduction that shares little in common with the original. Professional historians, especially those studying eras before the invention of the printing press, have always been cognizant of the need to check on the authenticity of sources, but in the modern age of the internet, anyone who uses digital search engines to conduct research must never forget this step in the historical process. Do not be gullible. Before you accept a source, especially a source found on an internet site, first do your homework, and do not use it until you are confident that it is an authentic primary source.

After determining that a source is authentic, the next step is to assess its credibility. Just because an eyewitness leaves an account of an event (thereby creating a primary source), this does not mean that this eyewitness offers a trustworthy testimony. After all, the source could have been intentionally produced to mislead future investigators. More likely, the source could have been an honest attempt at assessment that captured only a part of the truth or simply missed the mark entirely.

Determining how much credibility you give to each source is a judicious process. To help you reach your verdict about the credibility of a source, you may want to ask yourself some of the following questions:

> For whom did the author produce the source? Did the author intend it to be published and read by future investigators? How close – both in proximity and in relationship – was the author to the subject being described? Did the author have the skills and knowledge to provide expert testimony? Did the author rely on memory or on other sources while creating the account? How much time passed between the event and the author's testimony about it?

While assessing the credibility of a source can be a subjective process, by reflecting on questions such as these you will become a better detective and thereby become a better historian.

Beginner historians should not be surprised to find that even authentic and credible sources may not always converge with each other. One of the fundamental skills that historians must master is the ability to weigh, arrange, and integrate conflicting testimony. Fortunately, to a greater degree than newspaper journalists and CNN analysts who often must report breaking news as it unfolds, historians have the freedom and the responsibility to deliberatively reflect on multiple sources from multiple perspectives before rendering their judgments.

Another basic concept that historians must know is that the historical method cannot offer answers to all questions that might excite their curiosity. Consequently, when you create probing questions to study, you should avoid questions for which primary source evidence cannot be found, including, for instance, timeless existential questions like "what is the meaning of life?" or "what if" questions such as "would slavery have been abolished within fifty years if the Confederacy had won the Civil War?"

If your imagination draws you to these types of questions, do not abandon those thoughts and interests, but find ways to reframe non-historical questions into historical ones. For example, rather than asking the timeless question "what is the nature of God?", turn the question into a historical one located in time and place by asking "according to the Hebrew peoples at the time of Ezra, what was the nature of God?"

IT'S ABOUT TIME: THE AGONY & ECSTASY OF DATING

Another basic idea beginner historians need to understand is that history is a branch of knowledge that is fundamentally about time or, more precisely, timing. In comparison with science, history is a flexible discipline, welcoming multiple answers to the questions that it poses. There is one methodological rule, however, that is inviolable. What is this great commandment, this unalterable law? *Historians must agree that historic time is irreversible and, therefore, more recent events cannot be said to influence more distant ones.* To reverse the timing of events is to misconstrue the past.

Because placing things appropriately in time is so crucial to historical understanding, historians must become "dating" experts and therefore need to be aware of potential dating problems. Like real life dating, learning to date historically can be more complicated than it first appears, and can lead to horrific experiences if not done well. Thus, to help beginner historians create "history," here are a couple of recommended dating techniques that you may want to incorporate into your practice.

Dating tip one: realize that simply placing events on a timeline without referencing them to each other should be avoided unless your purpose in creating history is to treat insomnia.

The reason that making dates the focal point of your history is so deadly is because it is listless and boring, it offers little historical insight into the period being studied, and it actually can be misleading to your readers. Most readers of this work probably do not need to be convinced by our first two points, but regarding the third point, consider this. Placing events into a historical calendar can be confusing because there actually is no universally agreed on way to locate events in time.

The calendar that most of us use every day is the Gregorian, or Western Calendar. This calendar declares a year to consist of 365 days (except in leap-years when the number is 366) that are assigned to twelve months of 28 to 31 days in length, with the years being numbered in units before and after the estimated time of the birth of Jesus of Nazareth. Although this dating system is widely known around the world, it is not the only dating timeline currently in use.

To make the dating of events even more complicated, this current Gregorian calendar, which was recommended in 1582 by Pope Gregory XIII, revised an earlier Julian Calendar by refining how often leap years would be added to the calendar, and by moving the days of the calendar year forward so that the season of the year would be aligned with the seasons that existed in the year 325 when Emperor Constantine called Christian bishops to gather at Nicaea for the First Ecumenical Council. While Roman Catholic regions immediately adopted Pope Gregory's recommendations, generations would pass before non-Catholic regions accepted the Gregorian reforms. In fact, the last European nation embraced the new dating system only in 1923. Consequently, between 1582 and 1923, different dating systems were concurrently being used in different world regions, thereby creating potential confusion for those attempting to place events in time.

Here is one example of how duplicate dating systems can result in confusion. If a historian of literary giants stated that both Shakespeare and Cervantes died on April 23, 1616, she/he would be correct, although this statement, if offered without context, would be misleading because Shakespeare, in fact, lived ten days longer than Cervantes. They share a common date of death only because Shakespeare lived in England, which at the time followed the Old Style Julian Calendar, while Cervantes lived in Spain, which at that time had already embraced the New Style Gregorian Calendar.

This example reminds us that we need to carefully interpret distant sources, remembering that when arranging events in order, we must take into account whether the reference is using the Old Style (Julian) calendar, the New

Style (Gregorian) calendar, or some other dating system. Because this volume focuses mostly on British North America before 1752, the year England shifted from the Julian to the Gregorian calendar, in this first volume of the series we standardize all dates to the Old Style Julian Calendar. In subsequent volumes, our dating will be set to the New Style Gregorian Calendar.

Dating tip two: don't obsess about giving a label to the time that something happened, but explore what it was that made that moment special.

Time flows steadily, and history is about time, but this does not mean that historians must treat all moments of time equally. To illustrate this point, think about a moment that was especially meaningful to you, such as a day you hit a homerun, played in a recital, won an award, graduated from school, or suffered the loss of a loved one or pet. Now think about what you were doing three days before that event. Most likely, coming up with an answer to the second question is more difficult than remembering an answer to the first, even though each of these days contained the same number of seconds. If one were to construct a history of your life from your perspective, most likely it would be appropriate to give more space to the moments that were meaningful to you, not to some arbitrary times before those events.

To capture life in its fullest, historians need to be able first to identify and arrange meaningful events in their proper sequence, and then to connect the dots, developing thematic and geographical as well as chronological associations between these events. Through backward linking, historians search for the origins or causes of meaningful moments. Through forward linking, historians investigate the significance or consequences of critical times. In telling the story of a critical moment or in writing a comparative history, historians also establish contemporaneous linkages by creating parallel time charts and observing similarities and differences between whatever aspects of life pertinent to the topic are being investigated. The more dots that can be connected, and the more interconnected associations that can be drawn, the more visual, colorful, and precise the vision of the past will be. Piecing segments of the past together to make a meaningful whole is a complex task, but it need not be a dreadful experience. Indeed, having a romance with "historical dating" can have its pleasures and rewards.

IT'S ABOUT INTEGRITY: THE ETHICS OF CREATING HISTORY

History will continue to be recognized as a credible discipline only as long as historians are respected as people with integrity. As curious truth seekers, historians must never forget that their central task is to convey a truthful understanding of the past that is not intentionally misleading. Although individual biases may be difficult to remove completely, the proper method of historical inquiry is not to reach a conclusion about the past and then search for and carefully select evidence that will support that conclusion. This may be the central motive of political spin advisors for candidates running for office, but it is contrary to the motivations of Clio, the mythical muse of history. Remember, probing questions should come first, followed by answers based on the ensuing research; not the reverse.

To retain integrity and maintain credibility, historians also must avoid constructing a history more elaborate than the evidence warrants. While ethical scholars in any discipline would never contemplate fabricating data out of thin air, in the rush to publish an idea first, or to present an argument in a more developed stage than the evidence allows, some may be tempted to overstate their arguments. Historians with integrity should avoid this temptation. It is appropriate, and indeed a necessity, to present a thesis that forcefully and artfully articulates a vision of the past, but authoritative assertions should not exceed the evidence that supports them.

Plagiarism, another unethical conduct that historians must avoid, is often committed more by laziness and sloppiness than by intention. But whether committed intentionally or by ignorance, appropriating the ideas of others as one's own and borrowing expressions without appropriate acknowledgment of their original sources are serious ethical offenses that can tarnish a career and lead to personal embarrassment and even legal penalties. Avoid this hazard at all costs.

THE PURPOSE AND STRUCTURE OF *10 DAYS THAT CHANGED AMERICA*

Just as the United States of America is an unfinished nation, *10 Days That Changed America* is presented as an unfinished work. The text offers a model that demonstrates on nine occasions how human decisions and activities on a given day transformed America in profound and sometimes tragic ways. To complete the work promised in the title, however, a future historian will need to locate another epoch-making moment in America's past, and create a compelling history that explains how the events of that momentous day evolved and were resolved, and how this resolution itself produced ripples that affected the lives of ensuing generations of Americans.

Every page of this text is designed to motivate and train a future historian to complete this task.

To help transform students into historians, each chapter of *10 Days That Changed America* contains the following parts:

(1) A "DAY THAT CHANGED AMERICA" narrative of a trigger-point moment that shaped the course of America.

Each narrative (a) sets the stage for a decisive event in a prelude section by discussing causes and pertinent preliminary influences that preceded the event, (b) describes the activities that took place during this great event by telling a dramatic story of that turning point moment, and (c) assesses the consequence and significance of the event in a postlude section by outlining the immediate and long-term impact of that crucial moment on ensuing generations.

The pivotal turning point events included in this text help students to learn how historians can frame a story of the past by selecting critical moments in American history and then through backward and forward linking analyses, describe the causes and consequences of these times.

The nine turning point days presented in the text illustrate *one* way of framing the contours of the American past from its colonial beginnings through the era of the Civil War and Reconstruction. Some of the nine "The Big Event" days, like the day that Europeans made first contact with the indigenous people who lived on the island Columbus named "San Salvador," are symbolic days that altered life only minimally at that precise moment but over time produced momentous consequences. Other selections, like the day the colonists declared their independence from Britain, brought immediate far-reaching consequences. Some days, like the day the Confederates bombarded Fort Sumter, thus triggering the Civil War, are events well-known by most American school children, while other days, like the date that President John Adams decided to pursue peace with France, may be little known even by professional historians.

The purpose of selecting this particular collection of days is not to suggest that these are the only or even the most important trigger moments in American history. Indeed, throughout the semester students will be encouraged to critique the selections of these days, and to reflect on and present other ways to arrange events and retell a meaningful story of the American past.

Nor is the purpose of this text to suggest that historians must frame the past around events, indeed, single-day events, although it does demonstrate that it is possible to structure a history of the American past around a brief number of twenty-four hour time periods.

Rather, the turning point events included in this work are selected purely for pedagogical reasons. By studying the causes of these events, and by understanding how the consequences of these events altered the world landscape in ways that prepared America for other future turning point moments, students will learn how to piece together the segments of the American past into a meaningful whole, and by doing so, will learn how to become historians.

(2) A "Probing the Sources" section that provides a collection of primary source documents pertinent to the central narrative discussed in the chapter.

Because primary sources are the building blocks of history, each chapter presents readers with an opportunity to analyze for themselves pertinent sources related to the central chapter topic. Introductory remarks provide readers with the context needed to approach the documents. Questions guide students through an exploration of the texts as they learn how to extract clues from, critique the reliability of, and organize trustworthy information about life in the past from primary source materials.

(3) A "What Others Say" section that introduces students to the historiography of pertinent secondary sources related to the central narrative discussed in the chapter.

By examining excerpts or summary arguments from the works of historians who have studied the central topic of the chapter, students will be challenged to (a) evaluate and critique secondary source materials, and (b) understand how secondary sources provide readers not only with a perspective of the topic being studied, but also with insight on the life and times of the historians themselves.

(4) A "Looking Backward/Looking Forward" section that challenges students to embark on an individual and/or group project learning assignment that builds on content presented in the chapter.

At the conclusion of each chapter, students will be encouraged to develop their historical skills by exploring in more detail one segment of the past that was only briefly introduced in the chapter narrative. Each chapter will focus on at least one skill set that historians need to master. Recommended topics and suggested probing questions will guide students through this journey into the past. One individual exercise and one project-based learning assignment will be suggested in each chapter.

(5) A "PAUSE-REFLECT-THINK" feature interspersed throughout the text encourages critical thinking and active reading by leading students toward self-reflection and inquiry before inundating them with too many facts.

To promote healthy vision, optometrist Dr. Stephen Means recommends that avid readers and those glued to computer screens all day follow this simple 20/20/20 rule: every 20 minutes, gaze for 20 seconds at a distance of at least 20 feet away. The "PAUSE-REFLECT-THINK" feature inserted throughout this volume encourages this healthy habit even as it challenges students to develop another useful habit – the habit of adding self-reflection or "think time" to their learning experiences.

According to adult learning theory, students remain unmotivated and resist learning when they feel others are imposing information on them, but they become engaged learners when given the opportunity to apply their existing knowledge to new learning experiences. By asking students to periodically stop their reading in order to reflect on and react to a historical argument or unconventional idea, this feature promotes active participation even during the reading of the text.

(6) A "Suggested Readings" section that provides bibliographies of recommended sources available in print and digital versions.

(7) An "Online Resources" section that recommends websites that contain maps, illustrations, tables, and other types of information that is pertinent to the chapter. Although all of the sites listed in this section were live and approved by authors at

the time of the release of this work, because we do not control these sites, we cannot guarantee the quality of the content on these sites.

HISTORIANS AT WORK: HOW TO USE THIS TEXT

The following paragraphs illustrate how each section of the text is designed to build on and stimulate greater student interaction with the conceptual material presented in the chapter.

PROBING THE SOURCES: Moving from Story to History

In our earlier discussions about the origins of history, we made brief references to two sources, the Book of Genesis that is contained in the Hebrew and Christian Bibles and *The Histories* that was written by Herodotus and published around 440 BCE. To dig deeper into these texts, in this section we offer some introductory comments about these sources and provide short excerpts from each of them.

Scholars generally characterize the Genesis account as a traditional story that serves to express the worldview of a people. The technical term for such an account is "myth," but do not confuse this use of the word "myth" with the popular notion of an unfounded or false notion. Myth, in this technical sense, is a story with a point. It is a way to communicate a truth through story-telling.

Many consider Herodotus's *The Histories*, written by the so-called "father of history," as the work that created the genre we call history. As you compare these works, consider how the purposes and the methods of the authors of these pieces are similar and different. Based on your reading of these sources, what constitutes some differences between sacred stories (or myths) and history?

Document 1: Excerpts from Genesis 12:1-5 The Calling of Abram (Abraham)

> Now the LORD had said unto Abram, Get thee out of thy country, and from thy kindred, and from thy father's house, unto a land that I will shew thee: And I will make of thee a great nation, and I will bless thee, and make thy name great; and thou shalt be a blessing: And I will bless them that bless thee, and curse him that curseth thee: and in thee shall all families of the earth be blessed.
> So Abram departed, as the LORD had spoken unto him; and Lot went with him: and Abram

was seventy and five years old when he departed out of Haran. And Abram took Sarai his wife, and Lot his brother's son, and all their substance that they had gathered, and the souls that they had gotten in Haran; and they went forth to go into the land of Canaan; and into the land of Canaan they came.

[This translation was taken from the King James Version of the Christian Bible that was first published in 1611. If you would like to continue reading in Genesis or other books in the Hebrew and Christian Bibles, you can access these materials free of charge on many websites. A convenient site that allows you to select the translation of your choice can be found at: http://www.biblegateway.com]

Document 2: Excerpts from Herodotus, *The Histories*: Herodotus's Approach to the Past

Herodotus of Halicarnassus, his *Researches* are here set down to preserve the memory of the past by putting on record the astonishing achievements both of our own and of other peoples; and more particularly, to show how they came into conflict.

> Learned Persians put the responsibility for the quarrel on the Phoenicians.... Such then is the Persian story. In their view it was the capture of Troy that first made them enemies of the Greeks.... [T]he Phoenicians do not accept the Persians' account; they deny that they took her to Egypt by force....
>
> So much for what Persians and Phoenicians say; and I have no intention of passing judgment on its truth or falsity. I prefer to rely on my own knowledge, and to point out who it was in actual fact that first injured the Greeks...

[This excerpt is from Aubrey de Selincourt's translation of *The Histories*. For an inexpensive full text of this translation, see the 1972 Penguin Classics revised edition that comes with an introduction and notes by A. R. Burn.]

WHAT OTHERS SAY: Investigating Competing Historical Arguments

To create history, historians generally move from query to judgment. Specifically, they investigate primary sources for clues about life in the past, and after evaluating and organizing these clues, they offer a judgment of what life in the past was like. When working in the field of historiography, however, historians investigate as their primary sources the interpretative judgments of previous historians to find insights about the life and times of these historians. A central purpose of the "What Others Say" section is to help students learn how to identify similarities and differences between various historical interpretations, and to establish meaningful associations between these varying interpretations and the life experiences of the historians who rendered them.

Below are a dozen succinct statements about the nature or purpose of history that have been attributed to a sample of influential historians, philosophers, and literary figures that have contributed to the development of Western thought. The comments are listed according to the chronological year of birth of these authors.

Read and reflect on the judgments expressed in these comments by rearranging their statements into any non-chronological grouping that interests you. For example, you could choose to divide the authors into those you have heard about and those you have not heard about; into those with whom you agree and disagree, or into those you understand and those you do not.

After further reflection, select at least three figures that you would like to learn more about, and conduct secondary source research to find information about their lives and times. As you learn more about them, restate in your own words the meaning of their quotes regarding history. Can you find any connections between the ideas each author expresses and his/her times and/or life experiences?

Document 1: Selected Quotes – Historians on History

> The study of history is the best medicine for a sick mind; for in history you have a record of the infinite variety of human experience plainly set out for all to see; and in that record you can find yourself and your country both examples and warnings; fine things to take as models, base things rotten through and through, to avoid.
> Livy (64 or 59 BCE – 17 CE)

> Whoever wishes to foresee the future must consult the past; for human events ever resemble those of preceding times. This arises from the fact that they are produced by men who ever have been, and ever shall be,

animated by the same passions, and thus they necessarily have the same results.
Niccoló Machiavelli (1469 – 1527)

History consists, for the greater part, of the miseries brought upon the world by pride, ambition, avarice, revenge, lust, sedition, hypocrisy, ungoverned zeal, and all the train of disorderly appetite.
Edmund Burke (1729 – 1797)

Universal history, the history of what man has accomplished in this world, is at bottom the History of the Great Men who have worked here.
Thomas Carlyle (1795 – 1881)

To history has been assigned the office of judging the past, of instructing the present for the benefit of future generations. This work does not have such a lofty ambition. It wants only to show what actually happened.
Leopold von Ranke (1795 – 1886)

History has now been for the first time systematically considered, and has been found, like other phenomena, subject to invariable laws.
August Comte (1798 – 1857)

My object...has been simply to show our causes for national shame in the manner of our treatment of the Indians. It is a shame which the American nation ought not to lie under, for the American people, as a people, are not at heart unjust.
Helen Hunt Jackson (1830 – 1885)

It is the business of the historian to generalize and to guess as to the cause and effect, but he should do it modestly and not call it 'science,' and he should not regard it as his first duty, which is to tell the story.
George Macaulay Trevelyan (1876 – 1962)

History is too much about wars; biography too much about great men.
Virginia Woolf (1882 – 1941)

History is, in its essentials, the science of change. It knows and it teaches that it is impossible to find two events that are ever exactly alike, because the conditions from which they spring are never identical.
Marc Bloch (1886 – 1944)

Study the historian before you begin to study the facts.... By and large, the historian will get the kind of facts he wants. History means interpretation.
E. H. Carr (1892 – 1982)

The writing of history reflects the interests, predilections, and even prejudices of a given generation.
John Hope Franklin (1915 – 2009)

LOOKING BACKWARD/LOOKING FORWARD: Thinking Historically

An Oral History Project:

In one hundred words or less, describe your sentiments toward history. Then conduct an oral interview with an acquaintance or relative, preferably a generation or two older than you, and capture in a few words her/his appreciation for the study of the past. Compare the two accounts, and construct a compelling argument that offers an explanation for the similarities and/or differences in these accounts.

A Project Based Learning Assignment:

Gather with a group of your classmates who completed the "What Others Say" exercise, and ascertain biographical information (author's field of specialty, nationality, ethnicity, gender, and any other characteristic of interest) on each of the 12 authors. Reflect on your findings. What associations do you find to be noteworthy? What are some possible explanations for these associations? Based on the information your group collects, draft some tentative statements about the practice of history, and then critique each statement. What additional research could be undertaken to test the validity of your hypotheses?

SUGGESTED READINGS

A classic and useful work about history and the historical method is Carl G. Gustavson's *A Preface to History* (McGraw-Hill, 1959). For a more recent study, see John H. Arnold's *History: A Very Short Introduction* (Oxford University Press, 2000). For students interested in currents in historiography, see Norman J Wilson's *History in Crisis?*

Recent Directions in Historiography (Prentice Hall, 1999) and Mark Gilderhus's *History and Historians* (Pearson, 2010). For an excellent guide to writing and formatting, we recommend *A Manual for Writers of Research Papers, Theses, and Dissertations* that is published by the University of Chicago Press. Because formatting and citation rules are continuously under revision, be sure that you consult the most recent edition of this work.

ONLINE RESOURCES

The World According to Herodotus
http://upload.wikimedia.org/wikipedia/commons/0/05/Herodotus_World_Map.jpg

Primary Sources
The Histories of Herodotus
http://classics.mit.edu/Herodotus/history.html

A PREMISE AND A CHALLENGE

In summary, both the structure and content of this textbook supports the same end: to transform students into historians. The mantra of this text is *"create history, don't memorize it."*

If you are still not persuaded that:

> *historians exist not to memorize and regurgitate the past, but to create "history",*
>
> *the primary objective of history survey courses is NOT to teach students everything they need to know about history, but to help them become historians; and*
>
> *American historians understand that stories of the past include complex and fascinating tales of intrigue, adventure, irony, and fulfilled and unfulfilled dreams that offer insight into why Americans think and behave as they do,*

then we challenge you to keep an open mind as you read the following pages. Allow us an opportunity to present our case to you.

At the end of the semester, no matter what opinions you hold, we encourage you to send to us on the Green Publishing House website your thoughts about history in general and about this textbook in particular. Did reading this text change your attitude about history? Did it help you to become a better historian? Specifically, what pieces of the text did you find to be most and least helpful? What changes would you recommend in future editions? What other days in history should be included in order to revise and finish this work?

The insights you provide will be helpful to both future students and to the authors of this text. And for those who offer constructive criticism, do not be surprised if the next edition of this textbook incorporates some of your ideas.

Chapter 2:

An Uneven Exchange: October 12, 1492: Christopher Columbus and the Consequences of Contact

PRELUDE

In early August 1492, three small Spanish ships named the *Niña, Pinta,* and *Santa Maria* sailed westward into a vast and uncharted Atlantic ocean. After two months on the water, the food was rotten, the stench in the ships was unbearable, and there were no signs of land. The crew of about 90 disgruntled sailors whispered mutiny. Only a few months earlier, Christopher Columbus recruited these men to sail west with him toward the known riches of the east. At that time, experts laughed at this plan, not because they thought ships would fall off a flat planet, but because ships could not carry enough provisions to support the anticipated 10,000-mile or more trip from Europe to Asia. Believing, however, that the earth was smaller, and that the trip required less than a 3,000-mile voyage, Columbus insisted that the riches of the east were well within reach. Although each member of the crew had bet his life on the feasibility of Columbus's plan, after sixty days on the open seas with provisions running low, some had had enough and demanded that Columbus turn back. In a desperate move, Columbus convinced them to hold on for a few more days. His luck held out, and the crew soon saw signs of hope that they were nearing land, as he wrote in his journal,

> The men of the caravel *Pinta* saw a cane and a stick, and took on board another small stick that appeared to have been worked with iron, and a piece of cane, and other vegetation originating on land, and a small plank. The men of the caravel *Niña* also saw other signs of land and a small stick loaded with barnacles. With these signs, everyone breathed more easily and cheered up.

Several days later, at two hours after midnight on Friday, October 12, 1492, a sailor on the *Pinta* named Rodrigo de Triana spotted land. Columbus was not surprised. Everything was about on schedule. By his calculations, he had traveled slightly over 3,000 miles, and because of the southern route that he had purposefully selected to take advantage of westward winds, he believed that he was somewhere near India. With excitement, Columbus gathered his introductory letters from the Queen and King of Spain, expecting to find a grand Asian civilization with royal soldiers who would lead them to a majestic city. When morning broke, he went to shore bearing royal banners and men dressed in impressive uniforms.

But Columbus was met not by Asian soldiers. Instead, as he would write in his journal, the people "seemed to me ... very poor in everything ... all of them ... as naked as their mother bore them." Something was not right. Even though this encounter was not as Columbus expected, he held on to his hope of securing riches from the east. Calling the peoples he met "Indians," he spent the rest of this voyage, plus three later trans-Atlantic voyages, looking for Cipango (Japan), Cathay (China) and the territory of the Great Khan.

From the moment of first contact to his dying breath, Columbus refused to admit that he had underestimated the size of the earth. He refused to admit that he was visiting a continent unknown to Europeans. Columbus's theory about the size of the earth was wrong, but more by good fortune rather than by foresight, it did not result in the death of his crew. Notwithstanding his gross miscalculation, indeed, perhaps even because of it, on this momentous day in 1492 peoples living in different world regions came into contact. For good or bad, the two great worlds never again would remain isolated.

To understand Columbus's expectations, his journey, and the aftermath, you must know something about what happened in the years leading up to this event.

AMERICA BEFORE COLUMBUS

At the time of contact, the population of the Americas (comprised of what we now think of as North and South America) was approximately 70-100 million people, who were at least as diverse in language and culture as their Old World counterparts. The inhabitants of the New World represented diverse populations, some large, some small, some strong, some weak, some technologically advanced, some primitive, some highly urbanized, and some nomadic.

Despite these variations, there was one thing that all shared in common. For millennia, all the peoples of the Americas had lived in isolation from Old World peoples. This fact, perhaps more than any other statement about their ways of life, would determine their destinies in the coming centuries.

HISTORIANS & THE FIRST INHABITANTS OF AMERICA

Who were the first discoverers of the New World? When and how did they arrive?

PAUSE-REFLECT-THINK

In addition to seeking answers to these questions, ponder the questions themselves. Would anyone object to the wording of them? If so, why?

Because curious thinkers like to know the origins of human societies, it is not surprising that numerous scholars have attempted to provide answers to these basic questions. For many decades, most conventional scholars believed that the earliest inhabitants of the Americas migrated from regions of Mongolia (northeastern Asia) some 15,000 years ago across a "land bridge" near what is now called the Bering Strait that linked Alaska and Russia. These migrations probably followed the invention of new spears and other hunting implements that made it possible for humans to track and hunt large animals in this northern region. These first discoverers of the New World, thus, came from northeastern Asia by foot, bringing no domesticated animals with them except the dog.

Ensuing generations of these early adventurers gradually fanned out across the vast Western hemisphere, moving southward into Central and South America, and eastward into regions throughout North America. Recent scholarship based on DNA sampling and additional archaeological evidence has added to this story by suggesting that other Asian migrants may have settled in Chile and Peru before the descendants of those who crossed the Bering Strait arrived into this southern region. In this case, the first South Americans may have come from other Asian locations, not on foot but in primitive boats. According to this scholarship, in the millennia that followed these early waves of Asian migration, immigrant peoples spread throughout all of what is now known as the Americas, splitting into many groups each with unique languages, skills, tribes, and civilizations.

While there are historical truths in these statements, some people find these questions themselves to be awkward because the land mass we call the New World is not younger than the rest of the planet, and because, at least from one perspective, the earliest inhabitants of this land did not so much migrate to the region as the world in which they lived coalesced around them.

Scholars advocating this perspective warn us not to be misled by the verb "migrated" and by the noun "land bridge" that are commonly used in the conventional narratives. After all, the sixty-mile distance between modern Asia and North America was more than a thousand miles wide at the time of this so-called migration. In this geological era, an "Ice Age" known by experts as the Wisconsin Period of glaciation, frozen ocean waters expanded glaciers and lowered sea levels worldwide, thereby creating a huge land mass that connected the two modern continents. The islands that today sprinkle the waters between Russia and Asia were at that time mere mountain tops on this connecting sub-continental landmass.

For thousands of years, the descendants of the peoples Columbus called "Indians" lived in a frigid region – once all land but now mostly submerged – that geographers call "Berengia." As the temperatures on the planet warmed, a process that took thousands of years, the partial melting of glaciers unleashed waters that trickled into the oceans, slowly rising sea levels, which in time again separated the Western Hemisphere from Asia. These processes, of course, were so slow as to be unnoticed by the human inhabitants who for millennia had survived by hunting huge mammals that lived in this northern climate. Being dependent on these large animals for their food, clothing, and tools, they followed the game wherever it roamed. When waters again parted the continents, the Berengians located in the western regions became separated from humans on the other side of the divide. By happenstance, they, thus, became the first Americans.

Like humans everywhere on the planet, between the end of the last Ice Age and the arrival of the Spanish, the peoples living in the Western Hemisphere migrated, developed new skills, and created diversified cultures as they adapted to natural and human-made challenges threatening their survival. In comparison with Euro-Asians, however, the peoples of the Western Hemisphere faced several distinct disadvantages. Unlike Euro-Asians, for example, the peoples of the Americas lacked barley and wheat, grains richer in protein and easier to sow and store than American maize. Without goats, sheep, or cattle for milk and cheese, and horses or donkeys for transport, the pre-contact Americans also had fewer animal species that could be domesticated to support human sustenance and advancement.

Moreover, because climates and the cycle of seasons are more a function of changes in longitude than latitude, the East-West orientation of Europe and Asia made it relatively easy for Euro-Asians to carry domesticated seeds with them as they migrated from one side of the continental landmass to the other. The North-South orientation of the Americas provided no such advantage as crops domesticated around the equator could not be cultivated in more northern or southern regions because of dissimilar climates and seasonal cycles. Yet, notwithstanding these natural barriers, over a course of about fifteen thousand years the descendants of the nomadic Berengians spread across the Americas, creating a diversity of cultures that rivaled those of Europe, Asia, and Africa.

AGRICULTURAL TRANSFORMATION & ITS CONSEQUENCES

Between about 10,000 and 5000 BCE, humans in both the Old and New Worlds began to master the environment in new ways by cultivating the soil, selecting and planting seeds, and breeding animals that could help them survive. The transition from hunting and gathering to settled agriculture was a slow process, appearing first in the "fertile crescent" of Southwestern Asia around 10,000 BCE, later in China and Mexico around 7000 BCE, and then in India, southern Europe, Africa, and South America around 6000 BCE. Farming practices did not begin in more northerly regions until later, arriving in England and northern Europe around 4000 BCE and in North America around 1000 BCE.

Tilling the ground was hard work, as suggested in a line from the well-known Adam and Eve Garden of Eden story: "cursed is the ground ... in toil you shall eat ... thorns and thistles it shall bring forth to you, and you shall eat the plants of the field." Relying on farming for survival also made populations more vulnerable to disasters from drought and other natural calamities. Historians still debate whether farming cultures experienced better overall health than hunting and gathering cultures.

Generally, however, the advantages of settled agriculture outweighed the risks. While the transition to agriculture took place in different world regions at different times, in each locale the domestication of plants and animals resulted in a higher yield of nutrients per acre, which made possible more densely populated settlements. Agriculture also encouraged greater population growth, not only because of the potential for food surpluses, but also because the utilization of cow's milk and grain enabled mothers to breast-feed for shorter periods, which resulted in higher overall fertility rates. Larger populations in compacted settlements fostered the rise of villages and cities that reshaped societies in many ways. Urbanization allowed for greater specialization of labor, fostered the rise of new technologies, demanded more complex units of government, and encouraged cultural innovations such as recordkeeping and literature.

The more complex civilizations in the Western Hemisphere emerged not in North America, but in Central and South America. Geographically the largest of these was the Inca Empire, which stretched nearly 2,000 miles along the mountainous western coastal regions of South America. With no draft animals available for pulling, in the steep Andes there was no incentive to develop wheeled vehicle technologies, but this linguistically and ethnically diverse empire did engineer other creative innovations, including terrace irrigation, which opened the hillsides to farming, and the construction of an extended network of paved roads, which enabled trade and communication between the distant regions of the empire. Although nomadic hunters entered this area of South America some 9,000 years ago, the Inca Empire itself was relatively brief-lived, dominating the Andes for only one century until it was toppled by Spanish invaders in the 1530s.

In Central America, a series of elaborate civilizations emerged, peaked, and declined before the arrival of the Spanish. The first sophisticated culture to rise in this region was the Olmec civilization, which, during the last millennium BCE, constructed great cities with plazas and monumental head sculptures chiseled from volcanic rock. Emerging from the ruins of the Olmec was the Teotihuacan civilization, whose capital by 600 CE was the home of 120,000 – 200,000 city-dwellers. As one of the ten largest cities in the world at this time, Teotihuacan included broad avenues, markets, apartment complexes, public plazas, a stadium for games played with rubber balls, a drainage system of sewers, and a pyramid of the sun that towered over 200 feet high. Contemporaneous with Teotihuacan was the equally impressive Mayan Civilization, which built fifty urban centers across the Yucatan Peninsula, invented a sophisticated writing system and calendar, and acquired advanced knowledge in mathematics and astronomy.

During the thirteenth century, the Mexica (also known as the Aztec), swept into Mexico from their ancient ancestral homelands in the north, eventually establishing a capital at Tenochtitlan (site of present day Mexico City). Utilizing a slave workforce drawn from conquered neighboring tribes, at its peak Tenochtitlan was the largest pre-contact city in America, housing upwards of a quarter of a million residents. Like the Incas of Peru, however, the Aztec Empire would fall to the Spanish within one generation after contact.

THE DIVERSE CULTURES OF NORTH AMERICA

The pre-contact inhabitants of North America developed less complex but still significant civilizations. It is not surprising that societies that were more sophisticated emerged in the North American Southwest around 1000 BCE shortly after the practice of farming appeared in this region. The Mogollon and Hohokam cultures of New Mexico and Arizona developed water control and irrigation systems that enabled them to survive and flourish in this arid environment. Farther to the north in the Four Corners Region of Arizona, Colorado, New Mexico, and Utah, the Ancestral Puebloans (formerly called the Anasazi) built a number of major cities, including the Chaco Canyon settlement, which had structures thought to be astronomical observatories that were built by quarried sandstone blocks and timber hauled great distances on well-constructed roadways. This civilization, which flourished for more than a thousand years, traded elaborate crafts, including turquoise jewelry, woven baskets, and colorful pottery, to distant regions hundreds of miles away.

The Eastern Woodlands peoples lived between the Mississippi River and the Atlantic Coast. During the first half of the first millennium of the Common Era, an extensive trading network called the Hopewell tradition flourished in the Ohio and Mississippi Valleys. These peoples constructed mysterious earthen mounds, with some as burial places for important figures and others as sites for studying the moon, planets, and stars. Unlike the farming cultures of the Southwest, the builders of these great earthworks subsisted largely by hunting, fishing, and gathering the abundance of nuts that were native to the region.

Later mound builders, who flourished between 800 and 1500 CE, belonged to the Mississippian Culture. Utilizing large-scale maize agriculture to support an expanding population, the Mississippians built an expansive network of cities that encircled a commercial center called Cahokia, which was located at the confluence of the Mississippi and Missouri Rivers (near present-day St. Louis). Around 1200 CE, Cahokia supported a population of 40,000. Nearly six hundred years would elapse before North America would produce another city this large.

During its zenith, artisans working in Cahokia produced pottery, hoes, and stone tools that were traded to distant regions from Minnesota to the Great Lakes to the Gulf Coast. Mississippians enjoyed or suffered under a stratified social structure that brought wealth to some and enslavement to others. Unfortunately, violence also was common as skeletal remains suggest that three in ten may have died a violent death. In the early 1300s, Cahokia, and soon the other cities associated with Mississippian culture, disintegrated. This rapid decline and the relocations of peoples that resulted from it triggered lethal tribal tensions and the formation of new alliances and nations. Most of the North American nations that Europeans would encounter in the sixteenth and seventeenth centuries were products of this post-Mississippian ethnic reshuffling.

The agricultural revolution that led to city-building and complex organizational units in the Southwest and East did not spread to all regions of North America. The mild climate with plentiful rainfall that enabled lush forests, plants, and game, as well as the abundance of marine life, especially salmon, on the coasts of California and the Pacific Northwest made farming in these regions largely unnecessary. Farther to the north, the Inuit (or Eskimo) of the Arctic Circle sustained themselves by harvesting whales, walruses, and seals, while the inhabitants of the Subarctic survived by fishing in the summer, gathering berries in the fall, and hunting moose and caribou in the winter.

Life was equally harsh for the peoples on the Great Basin (Nevada, Utah, Wyoming, and Colorado) and further west on the Great Plains. Some peoples who lived near water sources cultivated maize, beans, squash, and sunflower, but most tribes in these regions survived by hunting and foraging. Hunting techniques included running bison over cliffs or catching them in corrals, tracking antelope and elk, and trapping birds, rattlesnakes, and toads. Because no horses existed in America between the end of the last Ice Age (when the American horse became extinct) and the coming of the Europeans, all hunting in this inhospitable environment took place on foot.

By the time of contact, the descendants of the earlier inhabitants of the Americas occupied two previously virgin continents. Having created great empires – some still surviving at the time of contact, others long deceased – these diverse peoples shared little in common other than being isolated for 15,000 years from the peoples, plants, animals, and germs of the rest of the world.

EUROPE BEFORE COLUMBUS

The men on Columbus's ships were not the first Europeans to spot the New World. Around 1000 CE Leif Ericson led a group of Norsemen from Scandinavia, better known as the Vikings, to become the first Europeans to settle on the North American continent. Establishing colonies first in Iceland and Greenland, they continued their western explorations by settling briefly in Labrador, naming this new land "Vinland" because it was good for growing grapevines for winemaking. Perhaps because of the bitter temperatures of the region, the Vikings left their settlements in America and returned to Europe with tall-tales about their adventures in this amazing "land of wine."

Although the Vikings may have been the first Europeans to settle in the New World, their discovery did not alter the course of Western Civilization. Indeed, their daring explorations to the west were soon forgotten, or at least remembered only in folklore that would become respected by future historians only after archeological digs would produce artifacts confirming the historicity of these tales.

The reason the Viking discovery, unlike Columbus's adventure five centuries later, did not trigger great changes in European history was because at the time of the Viking explorations the peoples of Europe were largely isolated, impoverished, and illiterate populations engaged in chronic local wars. Kings existed, but their powers were limited. During this era when small kingdoms fought constantly for dwindling resources, news of the existence of unknown lands to the west created little immediate value. Between the times of the Vikings and Columbus, however, Europe would be transformed in ways that would prepare it to make greater use of knowledge of the existence of a new world.

CHRISTENDOM AT AGE 1000

Europe in the year 1000 was largely a rural Christian society with few and sparsely populated cities. Other than Constantinople with its 300,000 residents, Europe had few cities of great notice. Rome's population was 35,000, Paris's 20,000, and London's only 10,000. Food supplies were sufficient to sustain feudal lords and their vassals, but not enough to support a large population of urban artisans and merchants.

True, political stability was on the rise, but the emerging commercial traffic between Christendom and the larger Islamic world was still in its infancy. In medieval Europe, workers lived and produced goods, not in vibrant cities lush with markets, but on *manors* – large estates of fields, meadows and forests owned by (or entrusted to) nobles. Other than the lords of the manors and their knights who fought for them, their clergy who prayed for them, and to a lesser extent, rent-paying freemen who owed little service to them, few producers held status and privilege. The great majority of those living on the manors were serfs – free peasants who pledged their labor and obedience to their lords in exchange for protection and a parcel of land to cultivate.

Typically, male serfs spent three days a week working the fields of their lords, and additional days during planting and harvesting. Female serfs also provided services for their lords such as spinning thread, weaving cloth, sewing clothes, keeping cattle and sheep, and churning butter and cheese. In return for having access to the land, serfs also paid taxes and fees to their lords.

Although serfs were not slaves, they enjoyed few legal rights. Moreover, because the lords provided them with the land, tools, and animals needed for their sustenance, serfs had little opportunity to move. Generally, the children, grandchildren, and great-grandchildren of serfs also spent their lives as peasants on their lords' manors.

TEMPERATURES, FOOD, AND DISEASE

Between 1000 and 1300, Europe's population doubled in size, rising from about 36 million to 79 million. To accommodate the growing population, feudal lords allowed serfs to clear forests and increase the amount of land in cultivation. The expansion of cultivated land, coupled with the invention of new technologies such as the horseshoe and the horse plow, increased the food supply.

Nature also serendipitously contributed to larger harvests. Between the 11th and 14th centuries, earth temperatures warmed, thereby extending the growing seasons in northern regions and allowing the introduction of new crops into these areas. Among the new crops introduced into northern Europe were beans, a crop that not only served as a healthy protein source for the people, but also enriched the fields by adding nitrogen to the soil. The cultivation of new lands with new technologies on enriched soil with longer growing seasons created a larger food supply sufficient to support a growing population that included rising numbers of urban artisans and merchants.

Unfortunately, the 1300s brought bad luck to Europe. As the Earth entered a cooling phrase, sometimes referred to as the Little Ice Age, damaged crops and shortened growing seasons triggered periods of famine, and with famine its corollaries, violence and disease. Difficult times turned worse in 1347 when merchant ships returning from the Black Sea arrived in Sicily with rodents carrying fleas infected with *Yersinia pestis*, a bacterium that causes the bubonic and other forms of plague – diseases that typically killed at least two in three infected humans within a week. During the next decade, the "Great Pestilence," later named the Black Death, swept across Europe leaving in its wake gruesome memories engrained in the nursery rhyme,

> "Ring around the rosey, pockets full of posey,
> Ashes, Ashes, we all fall down."

By the end of the century, Europe's population was cut almost in half. In some localized regions, as much as ninety percent of the population perished. It would take nearly two centuries for Europe's population to return to pre-plague levels.

The cultural and socio-economic ramifications of this century of death were dramatic. Religious motifs turned darker as people concluded that only God's anger could cause such pestilence; Jews accused of well poisoning were assaulted; and governments, without much success, attempted to prohibit food exports and set price controls on grain and wages, unpopular interventions that sometimes triggered revolts. The Black Death even affected Europe's dietary patterns. With fewer workers to till the fields and with profits of landowners in decline, land prices dropped and former agricultural fields became pasturelands, a transition that brought more meat and dairy into the diets of those living on the countryside, including peasants.

Despite the horrors of the plague and its aftermath, the catastrophe brought benefits to some survivors. Death meant both fewer landowners and fewer workers. As the supply of available land increased and the supply of laborers dwindled, the value of workers rose. Worker scarcity also made it more difficult for lords to impose taxes on serfs or to prevent them from leaving the manors. Sensing the weakness of the nobility, some peasants revolted, demanding an end to serfdom. Other serfs took advantage of the loosening social order and their newfound mobility by moving to towns and seeking jobs previously not open to them. The anonymity of towns and cities was especially alluring to ambitious women who aspired to leave the patriarchal countryside for places where both sexes could join guilds and could work side by side as butchers, bakers, and candlestick makers. The social instabilities that resulted from this century of death drew people toward urban living rather than away from it.

RISE OF TRADE, TOWNS & TECHNOLOGY

Towns and cities require food, people, and productive things for workers to do. In late medieval times, as farming advances increased the food supply and the erosion of the manor released hordes of willing workers from the countryside, Europe was poised for urban revival. Expanded markets were all that was needed for transferable goods and a transportation system that could connect buyers and sellers.

Between the 10th and 15th centuries, global trading networks that had been dormant for centuries were rebuilt and enlarged. During this era, two major events brought Europe in contact with the larger world: the Crusades (1100-1250) – a series of military campaigns initiated by the Roman Catholic Church to wrestle control of holy sites near Jerusalem from Muslims – and Marco Polo's adventure to the East (circa 1295). Assured by the pope that all their sins would be forgiven, Crusaders left Europe armed with shields, daggers, and swords. Although their wars failed to achieve lasting victories, the Crusaders returned home armed with luxury goods from the East that they discovered during their journeys to the Middle East. Spices from Indonesia, gems from India, and silk from China tantalized Europeans who wanted more of them. Marco Polo's overland adventure to China further enflamed Europe's appetite for eastern goods, even as it provided Europeans with a greater understanding of the geography and riches of the East.

Italian merchants took advantage of this growing demand by expanding commercial ports across the

Mediterranean and beyond, which exchanged European goods such as olive oil, wine, wool, and leather products for the newly discovered exotic goods from the East. To a greater degree than at any time since the disintegration of the western Roman Empire, cities began to play a major role in European economic development. More localized trade centers that specialized in the manufacturing of wool textiles also emerged in northwest Europe (modern day Belgium and northern France). By the 13th century, towns were appearing throughout the countryside of western Europe. Never again would the economy of this region rely so heavily on farming alone.

The emerging towns were dangerous and unhealthy, but were also islands of enterprise that brought together and produced a new breed of workers. Not lords, clergy, fighters, or peasants, the townspeople included merchants, bankers, artisans, and craftspeople who comprised a middle class positioned between the peasants and the landlords. They fit only awkwardly within medieval social structure, and were ridiculed as greedy and usurious by nobles, clergy, and peasants alike. Yet, as the members of this rising urban merchant class accumulated wealth, they also gained power, securing from local lords (and even kings) town charters of incorporation that granted self-rule and exemption from feudal regulation and taxes.

By weakening the authority of the nobility, the revival of trade and towns contributed to the state-building efforts of late medieval monarchs who wanted the right to levy new taxes and create standing armies. While not keen on taxes, merchants and other professionals dependent on trade needed access to the kings' military forces, which could keep their trade routes open. Consequently, many in the emerging middle class supported the rights of monarchs to collect new sources of revenue to sustain their armies.

Levying taxes to support military protection based on standing armies rather than feudal knights began in the Italian city-states of the 13th century, but over the ensuing centuries this practice spread to Portugal, France, Spain, England, and other emerging states. With the help of the merchant class, the new monarchs of these states limited the power of the feudal nobility, created more centralized taxation methods, enlarged the military with soldiers loyal to their monarchs, and attempted to enforce religious unity within their kingdoms.

With new sources of revenue and new knowledge arriving from distant lands, the new monarchs also introduced new technologies that would revolutionize their kingdoms. The invention or application of the printing press, gunpowder, and the compass, just to name a few, transformed European society in multiple ways.

By the birth of Columbus, Europe was a different world than it was during the time of the Viking explorations. The next time Europeans returned from a trip across the Atlantic with stories of a new land, news of this world would not be so readily dismissed and forgotten.

THE BIG EVENT
COLUMBUS AND HIS VISION

Christopher Columbus was born in 1451 in Genoa (Italy), the son of a wool weaver and merchant. At that time, Genoa was a thriving trade center in the emerging world economy. It also was a center of the African slave and gold trade. From his place of birth, Columbus learned firsthand about many ways to acquire great wealth from the sea.

As a teenager, Columbus went to sea, serving at least for a time on the crew of a ship that collected its wealth by plundering ships from other city-states. In 1477, he moved to Lisbon, Portugal, where he married the daughter of the governor of one of the Madeira Islands – Atlantic islands located 500 miles southwest of Portugal.

Although not a scholar, Columbus read a number of books on history, geography, astronomy, and religion. He knew, for example, that in 1470 a well-known astronomer named Paolo dal Pozzo Toscanelli had suggested that sailing west across the ocean would lead to a direct and shorter route to the Indies. Scientists of that day rejected Toscanelli's calculations, insisting that he had underestimated the size of the earth and that to make such passage would require a 12,000-mile voyage. Columbus, however, accepted Toscanelli's estimate that put the distance to the Indies at under 3,000 miles.

Using Toscanelli's estimates, in 1485 Columbus proposed that the Portuguese sponsor a western trip to the East, but King John II denied his request. Three years later Columbus sent John II a second proposition, which again was rejected. Being turned down by John II was a blow to Columbus because Portugal had been Europe's premier maritime advocate since Prince Henry the Navigator (1394-1460) began exploring the western coast of Africa looking for sources of gold. Finding conventional ships too heavy and slow for these voyages, Prince Henry invested Portuguese funds to build the *caravel*, a lighter and more agile ship that could sail in shallow and deep waters both into and against the wind. Henry also established navigation schools to train sea captains, and encouraged Portugal to explore and colonize Atlantic islands west of Portugal and Africa.

Despite Portugal's commitment to maritime exploration, John II rejected Columbus's plan because he believed a southern route to the East was more feasible than a western one. Because southern Africa was largely unexplored, no European knew how large it was, but most geographers assumed that it did not protrude much below the equator. If this were true, and if, as other experts said, Europe and Asia were separated by 12,000 miles of untamed seas, then sailing around Africa for the East was a safer and less expensive bet than sailing west. Moreover, John II already had appointed Bartoloméu Dias to head an expedition to sail around the southern tip of Africa in hopes of finding a trade route to India. At this point Portugal remained committed to finding a southern route to the East.

Disappointed but not discouraged, Columbus secured an audience with King Ferdinand and Queen Isabella of Spain, and pitched his proposal to them. Although the Queen liked Columbus, the royal advisers to the Spanish monarchs also insisted that the extreme distance to China made such a trip infeasible. Columbus and his brother then sought out the kings of France and England, again to no avail. Although virtually every 15th century monarch recognized that lucrative benefits would result from finding a water route to the East, each time Columbus made his appeal, local circumstances and his conflicts with the scientific experts got in his way. Columbus continued to peddle his plan, but he was a seller with no buyers.

COLUMBUS SAILED THE OCEAN BLUE, BUT WHY 1492?

Schoolchildren memorize the rhyme "In 1492, Columbus sailed the ocean blue." Unfortunately, many of these children spend the rest of their lives thinking that this is what history is all about. But to historians, more interesting than this fact is a question engrained within it: why 1492?

Although answers to this can be complex, one answer that can be expressed in another simple rhyme is,

> In 1492, Columbus had a dream,
> and what made it happen was
> a storm, a war, and a queen.

Let us explain. When Bartoloméu Dias returned to Portugal following his 1487-1488 voyage, he brought back some good news and some bad news. Early in his voyage, he discovered that Africa extended far below the equator. As he continued his southern journey along the western coast of Africa – a continent that seemed to have no end – temperatures began to fall, and the waters became more severe. After months at sea, his ship was caught in a violent storm that threw him off course and almost took his and his crew's lives. When land again was sighted, Africa was on the west side of his ship, indicating that Dias had rounded the continent. Naming the tip of Africa the Cape of Storms, Dias returned to Portugal with the good news that Africa could be circumvented. The bad news, however, was that the trip would be extremely long, and to do it, one would have to pass through the Cape of Storms.

John II of Portugal interpreted Dias's report as good news. With an eye for positive publicity, he renamed the Cape of Storms the Cape of Good Hope and recommitted Portugal to the task of reaching the East by sailing south. It would take another decade, but in 1498, Portugal would accomplish this goal by sending Vasco de Gama on a roundtrip voyage between Europe and India via the Cape of Good Hope.

Meanwhile, although John II was encouraged by Dias's discoveries, others found his report disconcerting. Dias had demonstrated that Africa was a gigantic continent and that a southern route to the East would not be easy, or inexpensive. This new knowledge made Columbus's plan appear less outrageous. After all, the experts were wrong regarding the size of Africa. Perhaps they also were wrong about the size of the planet.

Despite Queen Isabella's interest in Columbus and his proposal, she did not have the luxury to gamble on such a plan because at this time Spain was still engaged in a costly war against Muslims in southern Spain. But after a decade of fighting, in January 1492, Spain defeated the Muslim stronghold at Granada. For the first time in more than seven centuries, all of Spain was now under Christian rule.

Spain's victory essentially ended a period of largely peaceful coexistence between competing religions on the Iberian Peninsula. Later in 1492, Spain forced Jews under its jurisdiction to convert to Christianity or be exiled. Non-converting Sephardic Jews who had lived in Spain for nearly one thousand years were given three months to leave. In 1501, Spain applied a similar rule to Granada Muslims. Soon the options that Spain would present to all non-Catholic Christians living in Spanish controlled lands, including its territories in the New World, would be conversion, slavery, or exile.

The end of the war against Granada also made it possible for the Spanish monarchs to give their attention to other matters, including Columbus's idea that already had been rejected by them. Queen Isabella, especially, wanted to reconsider Columbus's plan, largely because both of them shared a common missionary interest in spreading Catholicism to every corner of the globe. In the end, Isabella and her husband rejected the advice given to them by their geographers and accepted the recommendation of Isabella's financial advisor who, at least according to a quote from Columbus's son Ferdinand, convinced them that supporting the enterprise "offered so little risk yet could prove of so great service to God and the exaltation of His Church, not to speak of the very great increase and glory of her realms and kingdoms."

As a result, in 1492 Columbus sailed the ocean blue.

CONTACT IN THE EYES OF COLUMBUS AND THE TAINOS

On October 12, 1492, Columbus set foot on the new land that he named "San Salvador," meaning "Holy Savior." The Taino natives called it Guanahani. On this day, two long separated civilizations met. Columbus saw naked people who appeared poor, ignorant, and in need of western technology, religion, and government. The Tainos saw in Columbus a tall, freckle–faced, and blue-eyed aging man, probably with a red to graying beard, dressed in elaborate but seasonally non-appropriate clothing. Columbus also saw in the jewelry worn by the natives some evidence of gold, but no evidence of armor or armaments. After meeting these people, the next time Columbus made an entry into his journal he wrote, "These people are very unskilled in arms…with fifty men they could all be subjected and made to do all that one wished."

PAUSE-REFLECT-THINK

Imagine what this encounter would have been like from the perspectives of Columbus, his crew, and the Tainos. What evidence can you present to support your assessments?

POSTLUDE
POLITICAL & ECONOMIC CONSEQUENCES OF CONTACT

The consequences of contact were swift, multifaceted, and enduring.

To support Columbus's inaugural venture, in 1492 the Spanish monarchs offered him three ships and a crew of ninety. Only a year later, after Columbus had returned to Spain with tales of adventure and displays of exotic birds, a smidgen of gold, and seven Taino servants, Spain granted the Admiral of the Sea seventeen ships and an army of twelve hundred men to accompany him on a second trans-Atlantic voyage.

His first trip was an exploratory mission, but his second, and subsequently his third and fourth trips, clearly included additional aspirations. Though the original objective of finding a waterway to the riches of the East remained, Spain also had on its agenda colonization and the extraction of wealth from the newfound lands.

If there ever was a moment of peaceful coexistence between the Spanish and the indigenous American populations, the honeymoon did not last long. Upon Columbus's return to the place of first contact, the island of Hispaniola, he learned that Taino warriors had killed the small band of sailors that Columbus had left behind to maintain Spanish presence on the island. Violence and aggression, mostly induced by the invading Spaniards, would become commonplace.

In search of wealth, the Spanish authorities placed a heavy gold tax on the natives, and when they were unable to meet the quota, war ensued. By the end of the 15th century, the native population of Hispaniola had been cut in half, and the survivors suffered under forced labor. The Hispaniola experience quickly spread to neighboring islands – Puerto Rico, Jamaica, Cuba, and Dominica. Within twenty years after first contact, the Spanish conquerors were reading the following proclamation to the indigenous island populations:

> We ask and require…that you acknowledge the Church as the ruler and superior of the whole world, and the high priest called the Pope, and in his name the king and queen…as superiors and lords and kings of these islands.

These instructions continued with the solemn warning:

> If you do so, you will do well...and we in their name shall receive you in all love and charity, and shall leave you your wives and your children and your lands free without servitude, that you may do with them and with yourselves what you like and think best, and they shall not compel you to turn Christians unless you yourselves, when informed of the truth, should wish to be converted to our holy Catholic faith...But if you do not do this or if you maliciously delay in doing it, I certify to you that with the help of God we shall forcefully enter into your country and shall make war against you in all ways and manners that we can, and shall subject you to the yoke and obedience of the Church and their highnesses; we shall take you and your wives and your children and shall make slaves of them, and as such sell and dispose of them as their highnesses may command.

The establishment of Spanish colonies altered Europe's balance of power as Spain's American empire quickly rivaled Portugal's emerging empire farther to the east. As early as 1493, the Spanish-born Roman Catholic Pope Alexander VI drew a line on a map of the Atlantic Ocean 100 leagues west of Portugal's Cape Verde Islands, and declared that all land occupied by non-Christians west of this line belonged to Spain. A year later, the monarchs of Spain and Portugal tweaked and formalized this arrangement in the Treaty of Tordesillas, a treaty blessed by the Roman Catholic Church that essentially divided the pagan world between Spain and Portugal.

As European scholars digested the new knowledge that was being reported by various trans-Atlantic explorers, some geographers (but not Columbus) became convinced that a large continent separated Europe from Asia. In 1507, the German mapmaker Martin Waldseemüller encapsulated this vision with a map of the world that included a new continent. The mapmaker named this land "America" after Amerigo Vespucci – another explorer who, unlike Columbus, argued that the newly explored lands were neither islands nor Asia, but a previously unexpected new continent.

Meanwhile, Spain continued to explore and conquer western lands. In 1513, Vasco de Balboa crossed the isthmus at Panama, and returned with news of a great new sea (later named the Pacific Ocean). His discovery added further credence to Waldseemüller's view of the world. In 1519,

Spain sent Ferdinand Magellan on a mission to sail around the world. Although Magellan himself died during this voyage, Magellan's ships returned three years after their departure, thus completing the first circumnavigation of the planet.

In the same year that Spain launched Magellan's voyage, Hernando Cortés, accompanied by 600 soldiers and many indigenous allies, approached the great Aztec empire that dominated Mexico. Welcomed by Montezuma, the great Aztec king who mistook Cortés for Quetzalcoatl – a god who had been prophesied to return from across the waters – Cortés and his armies entered Tenochtitlan, the gold-laden capital and the home of a quarter of a million people. Once inside the royal house, the Spanish launched a surprise attack against their welcoming hosts. The Aztec warriors resisted, and bitter combat waged for several years, but ultimately Cortés's technologically superior firepower, aided by European diseases that ravaged the native populations, brought victory to Spain.

A decade later, the Spanish, under Francisco Pizarro and his brothers, attacked the Incas in South America. Fortunately for the Spanish, in 1532 the once great Inca Empire was in decline because of a bloody four-year civil war that had not only weakened the empire militarily, but also had created deep-seated rifts between neighboring tribes and those loyal to the Inca regime. Ultimately, in South America as in

Mexico, it was the impact of disease and superior Spanish weaponry – in this case, the armed Spanish cavalry – that enabled an undersized European army to defeat its indigenous foes.

With the successful military expeditions of Hernando Cortés into Mexico (1519-1521), and Francisco Pizarro in Peru (1532-1533), Spanish domination over the indigenous peoples spread into all corners of the Americas. Owing to the vast deposits of gold and silver in these regions, Spain extracted great wealth from these lands by giving Spanish elites the right to exact tribute and labor from the natives.

Largely by the use of forced indigenous labor, by the end of the 16th century Spain was extracting over 250 tons of silver from the Americas annually, thereby bringing into Spanish coffers a tribute roughly equal to about one-half trillion dollars a year in current US currency. The ocean of new revenue that crossed the Atlantic propelled Spain into the wealthiest and most powerful European state of the 16th century.

THE DEMOGRAPHIC IMPACTS OF CONTACT

Contact also dramatically altered the population size and profile of the Americas. Unlike the later English who would colonize North America, the Spanish created and ruled an American empire largely without populating it.

During the 16th century, about 250,000 Spaniards immigrated to the Americas, a relatively small number when compared with the size of the native populations. Contact also resulted in the bringing of another 200,000 enslaved West Africans into the Americas. By 1600, probably no more than five percent of the population of the Americas was of Spanish descent.

Moreover, because only one in ten of the Spanish elites was female, another demographic consequence of contact was the birth of large numbers of children with Spanish fathers and indigenous mothers. By the end of the colonial period and continuing throughout much of Latin America today, peoples of mixed heritages, known as "mestizos," vastly outnumber both the indigenous and the transplanted European and African populations.

A more grisly and profound demographic consequence of contact was the wretched collapse in population of the indigenous peoples. This tragedy was partly wrought by invading Spanish armies. Even more devastating than Spanish bullets, however, were European germs.

Like the bubonic plague that had overwhelmed Europe, diseases such as smallpox, measles, chicken pox, cholera, influenza, leprosy, scarlet fever, typhoid, and malaria travelled to the New World from Europe and Africa and quickly spread throughout the native populations, which had no immunity to such diseases.

When Columbus arrived, 250,000 indigenous people lived on the island of Hispaniola, but within a few years, the vast majority were dead from disease, and only 14,000 remained. Similarly, during the 16th century the population of Mexico plummeted from about eight to two million, caused in part by war and famine, but also by the spread of infectious diseases from which the American natives were unprotected. Everywhere that Spanish explorers went, massive deaths followed. In some regions, upwards of ninety percent of the Native American people perished within a generation following Spanish contact.

Because the Americas lacked domesticated animals – one of the primary sources of disease-producing microorganisms – and because the indigenous Americans had not lived in dense populations for as long as the Europeans, fewer infectious agents existed in the New World than in the Old. As a result, while Native Americans also introduced agents that caused Chagas disease and syphilis to the Europeans, the health consequences of contact were not as severe for Old World as for New World peoples.

ENVIRONMENTAL & CULTURAL CONSEQUENCES OF CONTACT

Not all exchanges between the two worlds were negative. Because of contact, domesticated livestock such as cattle, goats, pigs, and sheep traveled with the Europeans to the New World, introducing new food sources into the Americas. Smaller food producing animals including chickens, rabbits, and geese (as well the less liked rats) also arrived in America aboard European ships, as did horses and donkeys, transportation animals that dramatically altered many Native American cultures. Returning aboard these same ships were American turkeys, llamas, and alpacas, animals that brought benefits to Old World peoples.

Plant exchanges also expanded the diets of people in both worlds. The Old World immigrants introduced fruits (apples, apricots, bananas, oranges, lemons, mangos, peaches, and pears), vegetables (asparagus, barley, beets, broccoli, cabbage, carrots, cauliflower, lettuce, oats, onions, peas, rice, rye, soybean, and wheat), and spices (black pepper, cinnamon, clove, garlic, and nutmeg) to the Americas, even as they brought back with them an abundance of native American fruits (avocadoes, papayas, pineapples, and pumpkins), nuts (cashews, peanuts, and pecans) and vegetables (bell and chili peppers, maize, potatoes, squash, sweet potatoes, and tomatoes). The cultural and dietary consequences of these exchanges were profound and enduring. Without the Columbian exchange, there would be no tomatoes in Italy, no potatoes in Ireland, no bananas in Central America, and no oranges in Florida.

Two New World plants that proved to be especially appealing and addictive to Europeans were cacao (the plant from which chocolate is derived) and tobacco. Cacao, grown and coveted in Mesoamerica for two thousand years for its pharmacological effects as a stimulant, intoxicant, and aphrodisiac, became an instant hit in Europe. The chocolate beverage produced by mixing ground cacao beans with water and wine became so popular and controversial in Catholic areas that in 1662, Pope Alexander VII announced that drinking medicinal liquids like chocolate before Holy Communion did not break the fast. Thereafter, Europeans identified this chocolate beverage as a "Catholic" drink, much like they viewed coffee as a "Muslim" drink. American tobacco also acquired widespread popularity in Europe as people smoked it both for pleasure and as a cure for lung disorders.

In sum, the mixing of germs, plants, animals, and peoples that followed Columbus's first landing altered the planet in many ways. Human life today is largely a consequence of this Columbian exchange.

PROBING THE SOURCES: Words from the Spanish Monarchs and Columbus

Included in this section are excerpts from pieces that were written in 1492 by the people most responsible for this maiden trans-Atlantic voyage.

The first document, "Privileges and Prerogatives Granted by Their Catholic Majesties," was given to Columbus by the Spanish monarchs, King Ferdinand and Queen Isabella. This proclamation not only details how the Spanish monarchs were willing to compensate Columbus for his daring efforts, but it also offers insights into what Spain expected Columbus to accomplish on this mission.

The second document is taken from Columbus's journal of his first trans-Atlantic voyage. Although it was not customary for 15th century sea captains to keep a travel log, Columbus wrote for his monarchs (and perhaps for future historians as well) a journal of his first voyage.

After returning to Spain, he gave this historic narrative to Queen Isabella, who kept the original and returned a copy to Columbus. The original manuscript was lost, but the copy of it passed to Columbus's eldest son. Although this draft of the journal was not published, Bartolomé de Las Casas encountered a copy of it while he was researching his own *History of the Indies* in the 1500s. Las Casas created notes from the journal, summarizing portions of it and transcribing verbatim other sections. The copy of Columbus's journal that survives (which itself was not published until 1825) comes from Las Casas's notes and transcriptions.

A generation younger than Columbus, Las Casas was not a close friend of Columbus, although Las Casas's father and three of his uncles sailed with Columbus on one of the Admiral's four voyages to the New World. Some scholars have suggested that Las Casas tweaked Columbus's words in order to make the Admiral appear in a more favorable light. However, because Las Casas spent his career defending Native Americans against the horrors of Spanish exploitation, and because his transcript of Columbus's journal includes passages that question both the moral integrity and the navigational skills of the Admiral, most scholars accept Las Casas's version of Columbus's journal as a close approximation of what the Admiral actually wrote during his historic voyage.

Document 1: Privileges and Prerogatives Granted by King Ferdinand and Queen Isabella to Christopher Columbus, April 30, 1492

> For as much of you, Christopher Columbus, are going by our command, with some of our

vessels and men, to discover and subdue some Islands and Continent in the ocean, and it is hoped that by God's assistance, some of the said Islands and Continent in the ocean will be discovered and conquered by your means and conduct, therefore it is but just and reasonable, that since you expose yourself to such danger to serve us, you should be rewarded for it. And we being willing to honour and favour You for the reasons aforesaid: Our will is, That you, Christopher Columbus, after discovering and conquering the said Islands and Continent ... that you be our Admiral, Vice-Roy, and Governour in them, and that for the future, you may call and stile yourself, D. Christopher Columbus, and that your sons and successors in the said employment, may call themselves Dons, Admirals, Vice-Roys, and Governours of them; and that you may exercise the office of Admiral, with the charge of Vice-Roy and Governor of the said Islands and Continent, which you and your Lieutenants shall conquer, and freely decide all cases, civil and criminal, appertaining to the said employment of Admiral, Vice-Roy, and Governour, as you shall think fit in justice, and as the Admirals of our kingdoms use to do; and that you have power to punish offenders; and you and your Lieutenants exercise the employments of Admiral, Vice-Roy, and Governour, in all things belonging to the said offices, or any of them; and that you enjoy the perquisites and salaries belonging to the said employments, and to each of them, in the same manner as the High Admiral of our kingdom does....

Document 2: Excerpts from the Journal of Columbus's First Voyage

[Friday, October 12]

Presently they saw naked people, and the Admiral went ashore in the armed ship's boat with the royal standard displayed. So did the captains of *Pinta* and *Niña* Martin Alonso Pinzón and Vicente Yáñez his brother, in their boats, with the banners of the Expedition, on which were depicted a green cross with an F on one arm and a Y on the other, and over each his or her crown. And, all having rendered thanks to Our Lord kneeling on the ground, embracing it with tears of joy for the immeasurable mercy of having reached it, the Admiral arose and gave this island the name *San Salvador*. ...

In order that we might win good friendship, because I knew that they were a people who could better be freed and converted to our Holy Faith by love than by force, I gave to some of them red caps and to some glass beads, which they hung on their necks, and many other things of slight value, in which they took much pleasure; they remained so much our friends that it was a marvel; and later they came swimming to the ships' boats in which we were, and brought us parrots and cotton thread in skeins and darts and many other things, and we swopped them for other things that we gave them, such as little glass beads and hawks' bells. Finally they swopped and gave everything they had, with good will; but it appeared to us that these people were very poor in everything. They go quite naked as their mothers bore them; and also the women, although I didn't see more than one really young girl. All that I saw were young men, none of them more than 30 years old, very well made, of very handsome bodies and very good faces; the hair coarse almost as the hair of a horse's tail and short; the hair they wear over their eyebrows, except a hank behind that they wear long and never cut. Some of them paint themselves black (and they are the color of the Canary Islanders, neither black nor white), and some paint themselves white, and others red, and others what they have. Some paint their faces, others the whole body, others the eyes only, others only the nose. They bear no arms, nor know thereof; for I showed them swords and they grasped them by the blade and cut themselves through ignorance; they have no iron. Their darts are a kind of rod without iron, and some have at the end a fish's tooth and others, other things. They are generally fairly tall and good looking, well made. I saw some who had marks of wounds on their bodies, and made signs to them to ask what it was, and they showed me how people of other islands which are near came there and wished to capture them, and they defended themselves. And I believed and now believe that people do come here from the mainland to take them as slaves.

They ought to be good servants and of good skill, for I see that they repeat very quickly all that is said to them; and I believe that they would easily be made Christians, because it seemed to me that they belonged to no religion. I, please Our Lord, will carry off six of them at my departure to Your Highnesses, so that they may learn to speak. I saw no beast of any kind except parrots in this island.

[These excerpts are borrowed from Samuel Eliot Morison's *Admiral of the Ocean Sea: A Life of Christopher Columbus, Vol. I* (Little, Brown and Company, 1942), pages 300-302.]

WHAT OTHERS SAY: Remembering Christopher Columbus

Few individuals have received such varied reviews regarding their contribution to humanity as Christopher Columbus.

About 300 years after contact, the newly independent United States of America needed a heritage that bypassed Great Britain. Thus when Congress agreed to create a new seat of government, commissioners passed over the name New Britannia (a title that would have been appropriate a century earlier) and called the land for the new Federal City the "Territory of Columbia." At this time, the name Columbus was a metaphor for the new nation that, like Columbus himself, courageously departed Europe in pursuit of a vision too grand to be comprehended by the less adventurous.

One hundred years later, at the time of the 400th anniversary of landfall, Americans venerated Columbus as the harbinger of progress, a man who sailed into the dark unknown despite the jeers of naysayers and who against all odds overcame the natural obstacles in his way to discover a virgin and underutilized land, bringing with him the benefits of Christianity and western culture to the primitive savages who lived there.

By the time of the 500th anniversary of contact, however, Columbus symbolized less American progress than American corruption and failure. No longer viewed as the discoverer of America – after all, how can anyone claim to discover a land already inhabited by 100,000 souls? – many Americans condemned Columbus not only for disregarding the rights of the indigenous natives, but also for setting into motion policies that led to the terrible destruction of both the peoples and the environment of the pristine pre-Columbian land.

Presented below are excerpts from the works of three prominent historians who have written about Columbus and his times. The first selection is from Washington Irving's *A History of the Life and Voyages of Christopher Columbus* (1828), a work that captured the heroic image of Columbus that had been emerging for fifty years prior to its publication. Although many readers remember Irving mainly for his fiction, including his famous American short story "Rip Van Winkle," for most of the 19th century critics considered this to be the definitive biography of Columbus.

The second excerpt taken from Herbert Baxter Adams's *Columbus and His Discovery of America* (Johns Hopkins Press, 1892) articulates the thoughts of one of America's most distinguished history professors at the time of the 400th anniversary of contact.

The final excerpt drawn from David E. Stannard's *American Holocaust* (Oxford University Press, 1992) expresses opinions more prevalent a century later around the time of 500th anniversary of landfall.

What attitudes and biases do you find in each of these pieces? What arguments do you consider to be most credible, and why?

Document 1: Columbus in the Eyes of Washington Irving. Excerpts from *A History of the Life and Voyages of Christopher Columbus* (1828), pages 3, 150-152

It is the object of the following work, to relate the deeds and fortunes of the mariner, who first had the judgment to divine, and the intrepidity to brave, the mysteries of this perilous deep; and who, by his hardy genius, his inflexible constancy, and his heroic courage, brought the ends of the earth into communication with each other. The narrative of his troubled life is the link which connects the history of the old world with that of the new.

[continuing with Irving's account of the landing]

No sooner did he [Columbus] land, than he threw himself upon his knees, kissed the earth, and returned thanks to God with tears of joy. His example was followed by the rest, whose hearts indeed overflowed with the same feelings of gratitude. Columbus then rising drew his sword, displayed the royal standard, and... took solemn possession in the name of the Castilian sovereigns, giving the island the name of San Salvador. Having complied with the requisite forms and ceremonies, he now called upon all present to take the oath of obedience to him as admiral and viceroy, representing the person of the sovereigns.

The feelings of the crew now burst forth in the most extravagant transports. They had recently considered themselves devoted men, hurrying forward to destruction; they now looked upon themselves as favourites of fortune, and gave themselves up to the most unbounded joy. They thronged around the admiral in their overflowing zeal. Some embraced him, others kissed his hands. Those who had been most mutinous and turbulent during the voyage, were now most devoted and enthusiastic....

The natives of the island, when, at the dawn of day they had beheld the ships, with their sails set, hovering on their coast, had supposed them some monsters which had issued from the deep during the night. They had crowded to the beach, and watched their movements with awful anxiety. Their veering about, apparently without effort; the shifting and furling of their sails, resembling huge wings, filled them with astonishment. When they beheld their boats approach the shore, and a number of strange beings clad in glittering steel, or raiment of various colours, landing upon the beach, they fled in affright to their woods. Finding, however, that there was no attempt to pursue, nor molest them, they gradually recovered from their terror, and approached the Spaniards with great awe, frequently prostrating themselves on the earth, and making signs of adoration.... The admiral particularly attracted their attention, from his commanding height, his air of authority, his dress of scarlet, and the deference which was paid him by his companions; all which pointed him out to be the commander. When they had still further recovered from their fears, they approached the Spaniards, touched their beards, and examined their hands and faces, admiring their whiteness. Columbus, pleased with their simplicity, their gentleness, and the confidence they reposed in beings who must have appeared to them so strange and formidable, suffered their scrutiny with perfect acquiescence. The wondering savages were won by this benignity;

they now supposed that the ships had sailed out of the crystal firmament which bounded their horizon, or that they had descended from above on their ample wings, and that these marvellous beings were inhabitants of the skies.

Document 2: Assessing the Consequences of Contact, an 1892 Version: Excerpts from Herbert Baxter Adams, *Columbus and His Discovery of America* (Johns Hopkins Press, 1892), pages 7-8, 26-28

Those faithful, finding eyes of Columbus! For now four hundred years they have looked outward upon the westward course of empire in the new hemisphere which he first opened to discovery and conquest. Our modern eyes seek in vain to arrest that steadfast, far-away gaze, which seems to be looking into a future beyond our own. In the radiant light of the four hundredth anniversary of the discovery of America, millions of men and women will look upon this man's face with curious or admiring eyes; but when this generation, and many hundred years shall have passed away, those "finding eyes" will still be shining on through art, and poetry and history, like stars in the firmament.

There is certain immortality in a great deed, like that of Columbus, which makes the doer, even though in many respects an ordinary man of his time, forever memorable. The discovery of America has been called the greatest event in secular history. This dictum may shock the ancients and startle the moderns; but let the mind of reflecting students range at will, through the centuries, back and forth in the galleries of human achievement, and determine if you can what single secular deed even approximates in grandeur and far-reaching historic significance to the finding of a new world on this earth, with which planet alone history is concerned. What are all the conquests of antiquity, or the decisive battles and great inventions of mankind, compared with America, time's noblest offspring? The passage of Christopher Columbus across the western sea, bearing the weight of Christendom and European civilization, opened the way for the greatest migrations in human history, for the steady march of enlightened nations towards civil and religious liberty. The discovery of America was the first crossing of Oceanus, that great and murmuring stream, which followed around the old Mediterranean world. Amid the groaning and travailing of human creation, men burst the confines of that outward sea and began to people new continents. I tell you, sirs, the modern history of Europe, with its long exodus of hungry, landless peoples, with its epoch-making wars, its revolutions in church and state, were conditioned by that one secular event called the discovery of America. ...

Columbus thought he had discovered certain islands lying off the eastern coast of Asia not far from Japan. He had no idea that he had approached an entirely new continent. ...

If Columbus had known the true distance from the Canary Islands to Japan, probably he would never have dared to attempt a voyage of twelve thousand miles upon unknown seas. The historic blunder which he made was simply an historic necessity, like many other human mistakes in science and philosophy. The great contribution which

Columbus made to human knowledge was that he demonstrated the existence of lands in the west, beyond the Atlantic Ocean and thus "linked forever the two worlds." Harrisse regards this discovery as the greatest in modern times. Alexander von Humboldt calls Columbus a giant standing on the confines between mediaeval and modern history and says 'his existence marks one of the great epochs in the history of the world.' Mr. Clements R. Markham maintains that all the discoveries made by other navigators, in the lifetime of Columbus, on the coasts of America, (except that of Cabral), were directly due to the first voyage of the admiral and should be classed as Columbian discoveries. Las Casas, a contemporary of Columbus, took the same historic view and said the admiral was the first to open the gates of ocean which had been closed for thousands of years. "It was he that put the thread into the hands of the rest by which they found the clue to more distant parts.

Modern critics of Columbus sometimes tell us that he began his maritime career as a pirate and sea-rover. So did the Vikings of

Scandinavia and the mariners of England. Spirits of the Danes and Norsemen! Shades of Drake and Hawkins! Who, if not pirates, were the original makers of Normandy and England? "Brave sea-captain," says Carlyle. "Norse sea-king–Columbus, my hero, royalist sea-king of all…." Columbus, we are told, was a kidnapper and a slave-trader. So were all the great voyagers of his time. Even Prince Henry the Navigator supported his naval college at Sagres by the slave trade. Are we man of the nineteenth century so far removed from the treaty of Washington in 1842 which stopped the slave trade that we can talk reproachfully of it in the fifteenth century? Columbus, it is said, scornfully, was a seeker after gold. What have men been doing since the beginning of the world or even since the Argonauts sailed westward to California in 1849? The poor Genoese pilot was ambitious. Ah, yes! Men do say that Caesar was ambitious. Columbus wanted, not a crown, but a vice-royalty in his island realm. What a craven he would have been, with his royal soul, to have accepted less power and honor than was accorded to Spanish admirals of his time.

Document 3: Assessing the Consequences of Contact, a 1992 Version: Excerpts from David E. Stannard, *American Holocaust* (Oxford University Press, 1992), pages xii-xiii

From almost the instant of the first human contact between Europe and the Americas firestorms of microbial pestilence *and* purposeful genocide began laying waste the American natives. Although at times operating independently, for most of the long centuries of devastation that followed 1492, disease and genocide were interdependent forces acting dynamically – whipsawing their victims between plague and violence, each one feeding upon the other, and together driving countless numbers of entire ancient societies to the brink – and often over the brink – of total extermination. In the pages that lie ahead we will examine the causes and the consequences of both these grisly phenomena.... It is the central purpose of this book ... to locate and examine the belief systems and the cultural attitudes that underlay such monstrous behavior. ...

For at a time when quincentennial festivities are in full flower to honor the famed Admiral of the Ocean Sea ... the ashes of yesterday, and their implications for all the world's hopes for tomorrow, are too often ignored in the unseemly roar of self-congratulation.

Moreover, the important question for the future in this case is not "can it happen again?" Rather, it is "can it be stopped...?"

Today, as five centuries ago, these people are being tortured and slaughtered, their homes and villages bombed and razed–while more than two-thirds of their rain forest homelands have now been intentionally burned and scraped into ruin. The murder and destruction continue, with the aid and assistance of the United States, even as these words are being written and read. And many of the detailed accounts from contemporary observers read much like those recorded by the conquistadors' chroniclers nearly 500 years earlier.

LOOKING BACKWARD/LOOKING FORWARD: Exploring the Consequences of Contact

A "Building Historical Skepticism" Exercise:

Survey history textbooks are by their length and purpose concise accounts that often introduce ideas not fully defended with evidence. Like all concise history surveys, this chapter contains some underdeveloped generalizations. For example, while discussing the consequences of the Black Death, the authors assert but do not elaborate on the statement: "Religious motifs turned darker as people concluded that only God's anger could cause such pestilence."

Scan the chapter for weakly supported assertions, and select one that raises your curiosity. Do some research on this topic and write a paragraph that either supports or criticizes the assertion. Support your critique with evidence from secondary or primary sources.

A Project Based Learning Assignment:

Exploring the Consequences of Contact: The world around a hundred years after the death of Columbus was vastly different than it was during the Admiral's life. Gather into a group and select an early European colonizing enterprise in North America that was not discussed in this chapter.

Options include: (a) the Spanish settlement at Santo Domingo [1496]; (b) the Spanish settlement at San Augustine [1565]; (c) the Spanish settlement in New Mexico [1598]; (d) the English exploration of and settlements around Roanoke Island [1584]; (e) the English settlement at Jamestown [1607]; or (f) the French settlement at Quebec [1608]. Conduct research on the origins, development, and significance of your selected settlement. Prepare a lecture that presents your findings.

SUGGESTED READINGS

Rear Admiral and naval historian Samuel Eliott Morison's Pulitzer Prize winning biography of Columbus, *Admiral of the Ocean Sea: A Lift of Christopher Columbus* (Little, Brown and Company, 1991), remains an excellent and highly readable introduction to Columbus and his world.

For a look at popular perceptions of Columbus throughout US history, see Claudia Bushman's *America Discovers Columbus: How an Italian Explorer Became an American Hero* (University Press of New England, 1992).

A more recent intriguing biography that attempts to portray Columbus neither as a hero nor a ruthless destroyer is anthropologist Carol Delaney's *Columbus and the Quest for*

Jerusalem: How Religion Drove the Voyages that Led to America (Simon and Schuster, 2011).

A thought-provoking work that seeks to explain why peoples from certain continents succeeded in displacing other peoples is Jared Diamond's Pulitzer Prize winning work *Guns, Germs, and Steel: The Fates of Human Societies* (W. W. Norton & Company, 2005). For a classic statement on the consequences of contact, see Alfred Crosby Jr.'s *The Columbian Exchange: Biological and Cultural Consequences of 1492* (Praeger, 2003).

ONLINE RESOURCES

Historical Drawings

Martin Waldseemüller's Map Naming the New World "America," 1507
http://www.loc.gov/item/2003626426/

Diego Gutierrez's Map of the Americas, 1562
http://www.loc.gov/item/map49000970/

Abraham Ortelius's Pictorial Map of the World, 1570
http://www.loc.gov/item/98687183/

Illustrations

Portrait of King Ferdinand

http://www.luminarium.org/encyclopedia/ferdinand.jpg

Portrait of Queen Isabella

http://en.wikipedia.org/wiki/Isabella_I_of_Castile#mediaviewer/File:Isabel_la_Cat%C3%B3lica-2.jpg

Sebastiano del Piombo's Portrait of Columbus, 1519

http://en.wikipedia.org/wiki/Christopher_Columbus#mediaviewer/File:Christopher_Columbus.PNG

Maps

Europe at 1000 CE

http://www.euratlas.net/history/europe/1000/index.html

Medieval Europe:

http://www.lib.utexas.edu/maps/historical/shepherd/europe_mediterranean_1097.jpg

Europe in the 15th Century

http://www.lib.utexas.edu/maps/historical/europe_15th_colbeck.jpg

The Voyages of Columbus

http://en.wikipedia.org/wiki/Voyages_of_Christopher_Columbus#mediaviewer/File:Viajes_de_colon_en.svg

Chapter 3:

Divorcing Church and State, October 9, 1635: John Winthrop and the Banishment of Roger Williams

PRELUDE

In August 1635, a great hurricane hit the fledgling city of Boston and the Massachusetts Bay Colony, destroying businesses and houses and uprooting thousands of trees. With its terrifying 130 miles-per-hour winds and 21-foot ocean water surge, the storm took the lives of dozens of English settlers and sailors as well as many of their Native American neighbors. Dubbing this the "Great Colonial Hurricane," historians believe that this Category 3 storm was the largest of the century, as well as the first to be experienced by English colonists who had never before witnessed such devastating natural forces. Just three months later, a legal "hurricane" hit the same area with a tidal wave whose ramifications are still felt today. The issues debated at that happening relate to your ability to tweet, to google, to choose where to go to school, what to learn, and to have the liberty to freely express your opinions about government, religion, and many other subjects.

    The date of that event was October 9, 1635. The place was a courthouse in Boston where the magistrates of Massachusetts Bay were summoned to render their judgments in a case against an indicted preacher named Roger Williams. On the accusing side of the chamber sat John Winthrop, the pious Governor of the colony who believed that God had called Massachusetts Bay to be a beacon of light – a "city on a hill" Christian commonwealth commissioned by God to set an example of holy living for Old England to imitate. According to the vision of Winthrop, the New World was a New Canaan, and the settlers of Massachusetts were, like the ancient Hebrews, God's chosen people sent on a unique "errand into the wilderness." Their task was to create a colony dedicated to the glory of God, a place where, in Winthrop's words, the "care of the public must oversway all private respects" and where everyone must learn "to do justly, to love mercy, and to walk humbly with our God." To Winthrop, nothing was more important than remaining obedient to this calling – not personal wealth, not family, not personal liberties.

    Appearing before Winthrop and the magistrates on this day was Roger Williams, a minister of the church in nearby Salem, a smaller coastal community about twelve miles northeast of Boston. On that day, Williams had been summoned to learn the verdict of the jurors who would decide his fate. Williams had committed no murder, thievery, fraud, or embezzlement. In fact, people considered him one of the most charming, intelligent, and upright citizens of the colony. The decision to be rendered on that day would have nothing to do with what Williams had done, but with what he believed and with what he had publically proclaimed.

What was this case all about, and how would the magistrates decide it? More importantly, why would they make the judgment that they did, and what would be the immediate and enduring ramifications of it? To answer these probing questions, it is first necessary to understand what bought these antagonists together at this time and place. Using a wide-angle lens, we will set the stage for this drama by galloping across the decades that had passed since the first meeting of the Old and New Worlds.

AFTER COLUMBUS: A CENTURY OF EXPLORATION & REFORMATION

Although historians continue to debate the timing of the ending of the Middle Ages and the beginning of the Modern Era, most would agree that at least in the trans-Atlantic world the century that followed Old World/New

World contact was an exhilarating period that produced relatively rapid and profound religious, economic, and political transitions. At least in comparison with previous centuries, the 16th century was an age characterized by increased speed, as improvements in transportation and communication seemed to make the world smaller and time faster. The great exchange in wealth that followed Spain's conquest of the New World altered the balance of power of nations, and encouraged the Christian monarchs on the Iberian Peninsula both to build global empires and to spread their Catholic religion to the ends of the earth.

The material successes of Spain and Portugal also motivated emerging nations in northern Europe (France, England, and the Netherlands) to compete for North American resources not yet dominated by Spain. A shattering of religious unity in northern Europe created tensions that initially delayed and then spurred European settlements in North America.

During the century that followed the death of Columbus in 1506, a variety of European nations explored the northern regions of the New World in the hopes of finding sources of treasure, but more often than not, these efforts met with disappointment and produced little financial gain.

To illustrate, just a few years after Columbus's first voyage, England sent John Cabot across the Atlantic (1497) to find either a water passage to China or an undiscovered source of gold. Cabot found a plentiful supply of codfish in Newfoundland, but nothing lucrative enough to tempt the ensuing English monarchs to invest in explorations of North America. Similarly, France commissioned Giovanni da Verrazano (1524) and later Jacque Cartier (three voyages between 1534 and 1542) to find either New World riches or a passage to known eastern riches. Verrazano succeeded in exploring the North American coast from current-day Maine to North Carolina, and Cartier found and explored the St. Lawrence River through Quebec, but like Cabot, neither found vast amounts of gold or the elusive (and non-existent) Northwest Passage to China.

Even Spain's forays into North America produced disappointing results. For example, Juan Ponce de Leon left Puerto Rico, which he governed, to explore Florida (1513-21), but did not find its legendary "fountain of youth," and Francisco de Coronado explored the North American Southwest (1540-42), finding the Grand Canyon but not the mythical Seven Cities of Gold that he was hoping to conquer. For much of the 16th century, the territory that later would become the United States and Canada was largely viewed by European monarchs as an inhospitable land not worth the cost of colonization.

But another 16th century development – the Protestant Reformation – would provide a second incentive for the European colonization of North America. For centuries, the Roman Catholic Church had dominated European religious life, but to its critics, the Roman Church had become corrupt, repressive, and indifferent to popular spiritual concerns. To these critics, too many parish priests neglected their pastoral duties, violated their vows of celibacy and poverty, lacked godly virtues, and were ignorant of the Bible and spiritual matters. Equally disconcerting to these critics were the tendencies of the church bishops and even popes to meddle into secular politics and to expand ecclesiastical revenues in order to support their ostentatious spending habits.

Martin Luther (1483-1546) was a German monk and university professor who was especially repulsed by these improprieties. On Halloween Day 1517, Luther nailed a list of 95 complaints against the church onto a door of a local cathedral. Many of these complaints challenged the church's practice of selling indulgences.

An indulgence was a church-approved document that promised to reduce or to cancel punishments in purgatory to those (or to the family of those) who gave cash donations to the church. The jingle used to market these indulgences – "as a coin in the coffer rings, a soul from purgatory springs" – inflamed Luther's passion because he did not believe that the pope had authority to release souls from purgatory. To Luther, entrance into heaven could not be purchased or even earned by doing good deeds. Rather, according to Luther, salvation was a gift that God freely gave to those undeserving sinners who had faith. Because it was human nature to sin, no one could be good enough to "merit" salvation. All who received God's free gift were justified "by faith alone."

Luther wrote his *95 Theses* in the hopes of reforming the church, not dividing it. The nail he hammered into the local church door, however, struck a controversy that would splinter Christendom. After 1520, when Pope Leo X excommunicated Luther for refusing to recant his views and burn his books, Luther used the power of the printing press to spread the messages that salvation was obtainable by faith alone, that the Bible (not the Pope) was the final source of authority, and that all believers could access God without the intercession of priests.

The tone of Luther's writings was blunt and severe, but it appealed to growing numbers of German princes and peasants alike who were outraged by the Roman Church's this-worldly conduct and neglect of spiritual disciplines. Luther's popularity also inspired non-German reformers to launch protests against Roman Catholic teachings. Among the most influential of these Protestant reformers was John Calvin (1509-64), a precocious French lawyer turned theologian who at age twenty-seven wrote *Institutes of the Christian Faith*, a systematic study of central reformation doctrines.

Fleeing the threat of anti-Protestant persecution in France, Calvin spent much of his life in Geneva, a Swiss city of 13,000 that became a haven for reformers escaping harassment in their own countries. Under Calvin's leadership, Geneva experimented with a theocratic form of city government that empowered a church court to punish sinful behaviors, even burning at the stake people judged to hold blasphemous beliefs. At this time, neither Protestants nor Catholics embraced the idea of religious toleration. Although disputes arose over the appropriate definition of truth, Protestants and Catholics alike were in agreement that it was the duty of godly governments to defend correct beliefs (orthodoxy) against erroneous ones (heresy).

By the mid-1500s, much of Germany and Scandinavia were falling under Lutheran influences while Calvinistic communities were appearing in Switzerland, Netherlands, and France. Although Spain, Portugal, Ireland, and Italy remained securely under Catholic control, the protests of the continental reformers loosened the bonds of Catholic traditions that had characterized Western Europe for more than a thousand years.

THE ENGLISH REFORMATION: THE RELIGION OF HENRY VIII & HIS CHILDREN

While the Protestant Reformation was inflaming the continent with religious discontent, across the English Channel another reformation was brewing. This English Reformation, however, was triggered less by the ideas of theologians than by the marital problems of an English King.

At the time of Luther's protests, Henry VIII was King of England. A loyal Catholic, Henry VIII wrote a book attacking the heresies of Luther, and for doing this, he received from Pope Leo X the title "Defender of the Faith." Leo X also awarded this designation to Henry's pious Catholic wife, Catherine of Aragon.

Before Catherine (the daughter of Queen Isabella and King Ferdinand II of Spain) married Henry, she was briefly married to Henry's older brother, Prince Arthur, whose untimely death placed Henry in line for the English throne. In order to forge a powerful Anglo-Spanish alliance, after Henry became King he promptly married Catherine, his former sister-in-law. Catherine bore Henry six children, but only daughter Mary survived infancy. Henry, however, wanted a male heir, and by the late-1620s concluded that Catherine could not give him this desire. Thus, claiming his first marriage was cursed because he had married a forbidden relative (see the biblical text Leviticus 20:21), Henry sought permission from the Pope to dissolve (or annul) his marriage with Catherine and marry Anne Boleyn, a sister of one of his mistresses.

The pope did not want to offend the "Defender of the Faith" Catholic King, but for political and moral reasons he could not grant this request. Consequently, in 1533 Henry VIII acted on his own by forcing the Archbishop of Canterbury to nullify his marriage with Catherine and validate his marriage with Anne, and by securing from Parliament the Act of Supremacy, which recognized the King of England, not the Pope, to be the head of the church in England. Later, to demonstrate his opposition to the Protestant reformers, Henry also secured from Parliament acts that reaffirmed Catholic traditions such as clerical celibacy and the importance of confessing sins before a priest, and set penalties from imprisonment to death to those who challenged these practices. Although Henry VIII did not like the theology of the Protestant reformers and remained a Catholic at heart, in order to get the annulment he wanted, he removed the Church of England from the authority of Rome.

Henry's marriage with Anne, however, did not last. The child Anne bore with him was another daughter, Elizabeth. Also upset with Anne for her independence and her

Protestant propensities, Henry allowed charges of treasonous adultery to be lodged against her. Notwithstanding the lack of credible evidence to support the charges, Anne was convicted and executed. The very next day, Henry became engaged to Jane Seymour, who within two weeks became Henry's third wife. Although the birth of a child would take her life (she died of post-natal complications), Jane did give Henry what he wanted: a baby boy. With the birth of Edward, Henry finally had a male heir.

Upon Henry's death in 1547, the nine-year-old Edward became King. As the son of Jane Seymour, a Protestant sympathizer, Edward VI was the first English monarch to be raised as a Protestant. During Edward's reign (1547-53), the Church of England became thoroughly Protestant in theology as well as church government, as it repealed Henry's anti-Protestant laws and replaced the Catholic Latin Mass with the theologically Protestant *Book of Common Prayer*.

Unfortunately for the Protestants, Edward died at age fifteen without children, and when England rejected the request in his will for his seventeen-year-old Protestant cousin Lady Jane Grey to be declared queen, his stepsister Mary, the daughter of Catherine, became queen. As the Queen of England and Ireland and as the wife of King Philip II of Spain, Mary was a powerful ruler with high ambitions that included purging England from the great sin of her father. To Mary,

Henry's great sin was having severed the Church of England from the authority of Rome.

To restore Catholic unity in England, during Mary's brief reign (1553-58) she executed 288 Protestant ministers and sympathizers, including teenager Lady Jane Grey, who simply had the misfortune of having been selected by her younger cousin Edward to be England's future queen, and Thomas Cranmer, the well-loved Archbishop of Canterbury who had introduced Protestant reforms during Edward's reign. For these activities, future Protestants would give this queen the nickname, "Bloody Mary."

Just as the Protestant Edward VI died without child, the Catholic Queen Mary also died without heir. Upon her death in 1558 during an influenza epidemic, the English Crown passed to Elizabeth, the only surviving child of Henry VIII. Although Elizabeth was a Protestant, she chose to pursue a more moderate religious policy than either her hyper-Protestant half-brother Edward or her hyper-Catholic half-sister Mary. As the "Supreme Governor of the Church of England," Elizabeth supported a form of Protestantism that allowed for the continuation of some Catholic customs.

During her long reign (1558-1603), Elizabeth's efforts to make the Church of England "comprehensive" enough to include both Protestant and Catholic customs won her many supporters. However, her religious moderation was despised both by pious Catholics who desired full obedience to Rome and by more radical Protestants (later known as Puritans) who did not believe her reforms did enough to "purify" the church from the "corruptions" of Catholicism.

GOD, GOLD, & THE COLONIZATION OF NORTH AMERICA

While the religious turmoil of the early 16th century distracted European monarchs from pursuing North American colonization, the end of religious uniformity in Western Europe encouraged some persecuted minorities to seek colonial sanctuaries across the Atlantic. In the 1560s, two separate groups of persecuted French Protestants (known as Huguenots) established brief-lived colonies in present-day South Carolina and Florida. Neither attempt survived, but the threat of a French Protestant colony in the region motivated Spain to establish a permanent colony in St. Augustine, Florida. From this base in Florida, Spain would better be able to protect from Protestant pirates the treasures that flowed on Spanish ships through the Gulf Stream waters.

If Catholic Spain harbored worries of a Protestant menace in Florida, England also felt threatened about the possibility of a Spanish or French invasion of England from nearby Catholic Ireland. To reduce this likelihood (or at least to rationalize the colonization of Ireland), in 1565 Elizabeth encouraged Protestant elites, including Humphrey Gilbert and Walter Raleigh, to repopulate Ireland with loyal subjects. When the Irish resisted these intrusions, the English ruthlessly subdued the island, slaughtering both militants and civilians alike. England's colonization model that was developed in Ireland – eliminating or relocating natives and replacing them with loyal English subjects – in time would also be attempted in North America.

Fearing attacks from Spain, Elizabeth also commissioned adventurers known as "Sea Dogs" to confiscate loot from Spanish ships and/or to find treasures of their own. To a few of these Sea Dogs, she also granted permission to explore, occupy, and govern land in America. In the 1570s, for example, Elizabeth awarded Martin Frobisher and the Cathay (China) Company the right to sail in any direction except east to reach the riches of the Orient. Consequently, between 1576 and 1578, the old Sea Dog Frobisher made several unsuccessful voyages across the Atlantic looking for China. Although he never discovered a Northwest Passage to the east, Frobisher did return from an exploration of the St. Lawrence River with 12,000 tons of glittering golden rocks, which unfortunately turned out to be worthless iron pyrite – "fools gold."

About this time, Elizabeth also granted a charter to Humphrey Gilbert, empowering him and his heirs to spread the faith by exploring, occupying, and governing any "remote heathen and barbarous lands, countries, and territories not actually possessed of any Christian prince or people." Gilbert attempted to create a colonial estate in Newfoundland, but upon finding the frigid environment inhospitable, he set sail for England to acquire additional supplies. Unfortunately, his ship was lost at sea on his return voyage.

Upon learning of Gilbert's death, Elizabeth reassigned Gilbert's charter to his half-brother, Walter Raleigh, another Sea Dog with colonization experiences in Ireland. Determined to find a more hospitable region for settlement, Raleigh sailed southward along the North American coast, naming the land "Virginia" in honor of the unmarried Queen Elizabeth. After surveying the area, Raleigh selected Roanoke Island (currently on the Outer Banks of North Carolina) as the site for his settlement.

Twice Raleigh sent colonists to Roanoke Colony, each time with insufficient provisions. With short supplies and fearing for their lives, the Roanoke colonists persuaded their governor, John White, to return to England to ask Raleigh and his backers for more life-sustaining provisions. White agreed. In 1587, leaving about 100 colonists behind at Roanoke, including his granddaughter, Virginia Dare, the first English baby born in the Americas, White sailed for England, hoping to return shortly with more provisions.

Because at this time Philip II of Spain was threatening a naval invasion of England, no English ships could be spared, and White was not permitted to return to Roanoke with new supplies. Although England won its naval war after defeating the great Spanish Armada in 1588, England's war with Spain delayed White's return to Roanoke. When White did return in 1590, rather than celebrating with his granddaughter her third birthday, White found the settlement completely deserted. All lodges had been dismantled, suggesting the departure had been planned in advance. The letters "CRO" – likely referring to the nearby Croatoan Island – had been carved into a tree, without the cross symbol that the colonists had been instructed to leave if they were attacked by hostile warriors.

What happened to the colonists at Roanoke who mysteriously disappeared? Historians have suggested a number of theories, but none is uncontested. What is acknowledged is that when Queen Elizabeth, the last surviving child of Henry Tudor, died in 1603, thereby putting her cousin James Stuart on the throne, more than a century had passed since Columbus's exploits in the Americas, and still there were no wealth-extracting English settlements in the New World.

Like Elizabeth Tudor, James Stuart (King James I) wanted to expand England's wealth and power, but unlike her, he aspired to imitate, not challenge the Spanish monarchs. Whereas Elizabeth released Sea Dogs to plunder Spanish treasures and granted wide authority to Protestant conquistadors to spread the faith by establishing great feudal estates in the Americas, James I bet England's future on the more limited and secular colonization efforts of joint-stock companies owned by English shareholders who pooled their resources to fund their North American business enterprises.

In 1606, James I awarded land charters to two groups of investors, one group from London and the other from Plymouth, England. The Plymouth group moved first, establishing a colony on the coast of Maine, but like the earlier English efforts at colonization, this colony did not survive. Then shortly before Christmas Day 1606, the London group sent 144 males (and no females) aboard three small ships, the *Susan Constant*, *Godspeed*, and *Discovery*, on a voyage to Virginia. When barely off the English shore, the winds stilled and the ships lay stranded in the waters for six weeks. Tempers and fevers flared, and rations needed for settlement were consumed. By the time the ships reached Virginia in late April 1607, thirty-nine of the original group were dead.

The survivors selected a site for settlement sixty miles up a river that they named James, in honor of their king. They selected this location for their Jamestown settlement because it had a deep-water shoreline, an abundance of trees and game, and could be defended from Spanish naval attacks. Little did they know that their greater adversary would not be Spanish sailors, but malaria-bearing mosquitoes that thrived in the marshlands of the low-lying two-mile long, one-mile wide peninsula. By the time a second shipment of supplies and men would arrive in January 1608, only about one in four of the original Jamestown settlers remained alive.

Even with the arrival of new supplies, surviving in Jamestown was not easy. Were it not for the hospitality of Powhatan, the powerful Algonquin chief who either out of pity or for reasons of military diplomacy shared with the settlers the secrets of growing corn, the Anglo death rate in Jamestown would have been even worse. When a severe drought hit the region in 1609, the famine was so great that during the ensuing winter some colonists resorted to cannibalizing the flesh of their deceased comrades in order to survive. By summer 1610, just before the London Company infused the colony with another round of supplies and 300 more settlers, Jamestown consisted of sixty sick and home-sick souls yearning to return home. Jamestown would go down in history as England's first permanent colony in the New World, but this recognition would have provided little solace to those original settlers and investors who lost their lives and their fortunes on the commercial venture.

EARLY AMERICAN MIGRANTS: GENTLEMEN, SERVANTS, & SLAVES

Several factors – insufficient company startup provisions, wasted time spent on gold-searching rather than crop-harvesting, the unhealthy environment, and a poor work ethic among the settlers – contributed to early Jamestown's debacle. One reason for these "starving times" was that many of the original settlers were either gentlemen, who expected to lead rather than work, or the servants of gentlemen, who came to do "men's work" that did not include field cultivation.

To correct these fatal and financial pitfalls, the Virginia Company of London sent over dictatorial leaders such as Lord De La Warr, Sir Thomas Dale, and Sir Thomas Gates to enforce harsh company laws designed to bring discipline to the colony. These laws threatened capital punishment for offences such as sodomy, adultery, stealing, illegal trade with the natives, slandering authorities, blasphemy, and even missing Sabbath religious services more than twice.

In addition to enforcing discipline, the Company continued its desperate search for profits. In 1612, a

Jamestown planter named John Rolfe experimented with a strain of tobacco seeds imported from the West Indies. His experiment worked, as the Virginia marshlands produced high yields of tobacco. James I despised the custom of smoking tobacco, calling it "loathsome to the eye, hateful to the nose, harmful to the brain, dangerous to the lungs ... the black, stinking flume ... resembling the ... smoke of the pit [of hell]." Notwithstanding the King's disgust of tobacco, the company investors celebrated because they finally discovered a profitable cash crop, "Virginia gold," that could grow in Virginia soil.

In another innovative move, in 1618 the company managers approved sweeping reforms designed to make life in Virginia more bearable for the colonists and more profitable for the stockholders. The company abolished the harsh laws previously imposed on the settlers, and allowed the planters to elect members to a House of Burgesses that was given limited authority to make laws for the colony. Initially, all men aged seventeen or older could vote, although a half-century later this right was limited only to landowning adult men. The company also granted every Anglo living in the colony 100 acres of company land. Moreover, to attract more workers to Virginia, the company established a "headright" system that granted fifty acres of land to every new settler or to anyone in England who would pay the passage of an immigrant to

Virginia. In return, the owners of this free land agreed to pay a "quitrent"(a small annual fee)to the investors. This reform encouraged families, including women and children, to migrate to Virginia together because the larger the family unit, the larger the awarded land grant. Additionally, to supply the colonial men with wives, in 1619 the company recruited and sent to Virginia shiploads of English women who agreed to be auctioned to planters who would pay the transit costs of their future wives.

These reforms had an immediate impact. After more than a decade of attempted settlements, in early 1618 the Anglo population in Virginia included only about 400 men and a few women. Within a couple of years, however, Virginia's population tripled in size, and included more than a hundred women, making possible for the first time significant growth of a naturally born English population.

Although the population surge and the new revenues from tobacco would come too late to bring profits to the original stockholders, these changes did transform early Virginia in fundamental ways. To illustrate, the headright system, coupled with the prospect of cultivating a profitable crop, created a group of ambitious large estate owners. All that stood between the land they owned and capital to be gained through tobacco was a labor force that could cultivate the fields. Because the Virginian planters were unsuccessful in forcing local Indians to do this work, they needed to find other labor sources. By the second decade of the colony, these planters increasingly turned to "indentured servants" to perform this much-needed labor.

Indentured servants were bound laborers who, in exchange for the price of passage, legally committed themselves to work a set number of years for their masters. Most of these indentured servants were young males (only one in four was female) between the ages of fifteen and twenty-four, who typically came from England's laboring classes in London, Liverpool, and Bristol. During the 17th century, about three-in-four English migrants to Virginia originally arrived as indentured servants who, being unable to afford their own passage, exchanged four to seven years of their youth for the right to live in America.

While servants, they worked for their masters 24/7. They could not leave their masters without permission, and could not marry or have families. Female servants becoming pregnant before the expiration date of the contract received fines, whippings, or additional years of service added to their contracts. After the contracted years of servitude were complete, servants of both sexes were released from their masters, becoming free people able to compete in the workforce and marry. Because of the relative scarcity of women in the colony, and because few of them had nearby fathers or other relatives telling them whom to marry, women had considerable latitude in the selection of their husbands, and therefore more power than many southern women would enjoy in future centuries. Unfortunately, nearly half of the indentured servants died before they received their freedom, and few ever acquired the abundant land and wealth that had been promised to them by their recruiters.

The great majority of 17th century Virginia servants came of their own free will, although in time, another source of "non-free" laborers would be imported from Africa to work the tobacco plantations. We know from an entry in John Rolfe's journal that the first Africans were purchased by Virginia planters in 1619. Historians still debate whether these African workers were sold as indentured servants or as slaves who had little hope for future freedom and whose offspring also became the property of their masters. The first laws passed by the House of Burgesses distinguishing legal indentured servitude from slavery were not introduced until the 1660s. Before this time, serving a master was not associated with race, as peoples of all ethnicities were legally bound, at least for a period, to those who purchased them. However, because the sale price of servants varied by race and sex, with African females being the most expensive, followed by African men, English men, and finally English women, it is likely that slavery existed in custom if not in Virginia law at least as early as the 1640s.

In the 18th century, slavery became a big business in Virginia, but for most of the 17th century, it remained a rare phenomenon. At mid-century, Virginia's population had grown to about 15,000, but of this number, only about three hundred were Africans. At least one African, Francis Payne, had accumulated sufficient wealth to purchase both his own freedom and personal servants as well, but this advancement from servant to master was rare, especially for Africans. For most of the century, the majority of Virginia workers were males recruited from England's laboring classes who spent their youth in servitude. They lived difficult lives and often died young, but at least cherished a hope for freedom.

The introduction of the headright system and the cultivation of tobacco also made relations worse between the English settlers and the Native Americans who lived in the region. In the early years of English settlement, Powhatan would have found the English colonists to be arrogant, impractical, and strange, but not particularly threatening. From Powhatan's perspective, the English disrespectfully reproached the protective gods known to the Algonquian peoples and asserted the superiority of their Christian god, but then fell sick and died off in large numbers in the swampy marshlands in which they chose to live. They foolishly asserted that the Algonquin must serve some distant English king who had no power over them, and even expected their welcoming hosts to feed them with food produced and needed for Algonquin survival. They wore gaudy and inappropriate clothing and sailed in vessels that could challenge the ocean waves, but needed to be taught how to construct simple canoes that could transport them up, down, and across the streams and rivers that separated their villages. They wasted time looking for precious metals, a fantasy appropriate for children, but did not seem to recognize that these treasures were not native to the land. They traveled across the great waters with only men and boys without giving forethought as to whom would do the "women's work" that Powhatan considered to be necessary for survival. Who was to cultivate their fields? Who would prepare their food and feed them? Who would procreate their race? How could they have been so dull as to have not considered these basic things before they left their homes?

Yet, despite their ignorance and shortcomings, the English had one thing that the powerful Powhatan appreciated: advanced weaponry. Although English muskets could not strike as quickly as the Indian bow, the English had a noise-making weapon that could terrorize and kill. As king over a large empire of nations, some of whom sometimes rebelled against his authority, Powhatan was wise enough to understand that forging an alliance with this tiny band of sickly foreigners could provide him with access to military hardware that could help him maintain control over his primary rivals – Indian nations that did not bow to his sovereignty.

Despite periodic episodes of violence, Powhatan tried peacefully to coexist with the English, using all of the traditional diplomacy available to him to forge a lasting alliance. When a brash warrior calling himself Captain John Smith – one of the few English settlers who seemed to understand the art of war – had the audacity to make demands to the Algonquin king, Powhatan conducted a ritual ceremony of adoption by first threatening Smith's life and then having his 12 or 13 year old daughter, Princess Pocahontas, request that the soldier's life be spared. The purpose of the ceremony was to extend friendship to Smith by adopting him into the tribe, expecting from him in return gratitude and allegiance to the one who gave him back his life.

Six years later, when Pocahontas was a young woman, Powhatan attempted an alliance with the English through marriage. Just as European monarchs used marriage to cement foreign alliances (e.g., Ferdinand's marriage to Isabella, Henry VIII's marriage to Catherine of Aragon, Philip II's marriage to Mary Tudor, Charles I's marriage to Henrietta Maria), Powhatan allowed Princess Pocahontas to marry the wealthy and influential Virginia planter John Rolfe, convert to his religion, bear his son, and travel with him to England, where she was paraded around and presented as a paragon of the civilizing influences of Christianity upon a savage people. Powhatan no doubt experienced great pain when Rolfe returned to Virginia with the tragic news that Pocahontas had contracted a European disease (likely smallpox or measles) and died during her stay in England. With the marriage alliance severed, and with English intrusions into Algonquin lands increasing, tensions between the Americans and English amplified. Yet, through his death in 1618, Powhatan resisted the arguments of his more hawkish advisors to eliminate the English settlers in Virginia.

The delicate truce between the two peoples dissolved after Powhatan's more militant younger brother, Opechancanough, assumed tribal leadership. Upon his order, in March 1622 Algonquin warriors attacked Jamestown, in a single day eliminating almost one-third of Virginia's Anglo population. English retaliations would be even more deadly, and by 1644 with the capture and execution of Opechancanough, Powhatan's once great confederation would be utterly crushed. Nonetheless, the surprise attack of 1622 stunned the Virginia Company investors and King James, who promptly ordered an investigation into the safety of English subjects in the Chesapeake. After the horrid conditions of the settlers became exposed, in 1624 James I revoked the company charter, a first step toward turning Virginia into a royal colony. Virginia would survive as the first permanent English colony in the New World, but to its original investors, who lost the equivalent of $15 million current dollars on the venture, and to the 8,000 colonists who left England between 1606 and 1624 to live in Virginia, five in six of whom either perished there or promptly returned home to safety, Virginia would be remembered as a financial bust and a death-trap.

In 1632, George Calvert, an advisor to Charles I who held the title Lord Baltimore, asked the English monarch for the right to establish a colony in the Chesapeake. As an astute Catholic businessman and politician, Lord Baltimore had the ambition of turning this colony into a successful real estate venture that also would serve as a location where English Catholics could worship without the threat of persecution. George Calvert died before he could make this dream a success, but Charles I did award Cecilius Calvert, George's son, a charter to establish Maryland, named to honor King Charles' Catholic wife, Henrietta Maria. The charter granted to Lord Baltimore and his heirs a vast estate comprising 12 million acres, and bestowed upon him the feudal powers to wage war, collect taxes, and establish a colonial nobility.

Lord Baltimore used his substantial authority to grant large estates to his relatives and other English aristocrats. Because the financial success of the venture depended on attracting a large supply of workers, Protestants as well as Catholics were welcomed, and from the beginning, more Protestants than Catholics populated Maryland, although most of the landed elites were Catholic.

In 1634, two ships, the *Ark* and the *Dove*, brought two to three hundred colonists with ample provisions to establish the village of St. Mary's, also diplomatically named after the Catholic queen. Although Lord Baltimore retained the authority to distribute land, as in Virginia, over time he permitted the creation of a representative assessment called the House of Delegates, approved a "headright" system that awarded generous tracts of land to the settlers, and encouraged the cultivation of tobacco harvested by indentured servants. By the late 17th century, slaves imported from Africa.

To protect the rights of Catholics from the growing Protestant majorities, in 1649 Lord Baltimore supported approval of the Maryland Act of Toleration. This act assured freedom of worship for all Christians who acknowledged the triune God, although the act retained the death penalty for those who denied the divinity of Jesus or the Dogma of the Trinity (the idea that God is of one essence and three persons: Father, Son, and Holy Spirit). Although a historic act ahead of its time, the Maryland experiment in limited religious toleration did not last, as the law was repealed by Protestant majorities in 1654, reinstated in 1658, and repealed again in 1692.

Economic, geographic, and religious tensions invoked mid-17th century violence in the Chesapeake. For most years between 1642 and 1676, Sir William Berkeley served as royal governor of Virginia. Fueled by massive migrations from England, the population of Virginia soared from a colony of about 10,000 in 1640 to 50,000 in 1670. Among these new migrants were considerable numbers of well-to-do men and women from England's social elites that Governor Berkeley had recruited by offering them large estates and political authority in Virginia's wealthy tidewater (eastern) regions. Settlers in Virginia's backcountry (western) regions resented the power of the governor and his tidewater aristocratic allies. In 1675, when hostile Indians threatened English colonists on the western Virginia frontier, a group of backcountry settlers led by Nathaniel Bacon demanded that Berkeley raise a militia to remove the Indians from the region. After Berkeley ignored this request, Bacon raised his own militia of a thousand Virginians, including former indentured servants and Africans from the lowering classes, and used it not only against the Indians on the frontier but also against Berkeley's government in Jamestown. Bacon's death prevented him from overthrowing the royal governor, but Bacon's Rebellion revealed the brewing bitter tensions that divided not only the

English and Native American populations, but also the tidewater aristocratic estate holders and the less stable and largely landless backcountry Virginians who felt betrayed by the eastern royal establishment.

THE BIG EVENT
PURITANS, PILGRIMS, & THE SETTLEMENT OF NEW ENGLAND

During the long reign of Elizabeth (1558-1603), radical Protestants, those who felt the queen was not doing enough to purify the Church of England from corruption, acquired the derogatory title "Puritans" from their foes. Although they did not choose the name, they did share a passion to cleanse the Church of England from those Catholic traditions that they did not think were supported by the Bible.

Most of these Puritans embraced five Calvinistic doctrines (meaning ideas advocated by the reformer John Calvin) that can be recalled by remembering the word TULIP. These central tenets of faith include:

T—Total depravity of humankind, which means all humans are guilty of sin from birth;

U—Unmerited grace, which means salvation cannot be earned by doing good deeds;

L—Limited atonement, which means that Jesus died for the sins of those whom God ordained (predestined) to be included in the family of God;

I—Irresistible grace, which means that those predestined by God for salvation will find the grace of God irresistible and thus will not reject this divine gift;

P—Perseverance of the saints, which means that the predestined who receive the gift of God's grace will remain faithful and not fall from grace (i.e., once saved, always saved).

While accepting these common faith assumptions, Puritans disagreed on a number of other issues, including whether the Church of England was so corrupt that it was no longer God's church. Most Puritans asserted that while God was displeased with the government and impurities of the Church of England, God still loved the church and wanted its members to work within it to reform it into the church that God wanted it to be.

A minority of more extreme Puritans, however, believed that the Church of England was so corrupt that it should no longer be viewed as a church of God. To these Puritans known as Separatists, true Christians were called to denounce the evils of the Church of England and to separate from it into congregations believers fully committed to follow the divine commands contained in the Bible.

One group of Separatist Puritans lived in Scrooby, England, a small community located about 150 miles north of London. As Separatists, they denounced the evils of the Church of England, and for this, they were persecuted by the local townsfolk.

To escape this persecution, around 1607 these Separatist Scroobyites began moving in small groups to Leyden, Holland, a Protestant town where they would be allowed to worship without the threat of persecution. Although they appreciated this liberty, in Leyden they were prohibited from craft guilds and thus had to take poorly paying jobs. Moreover, over time they grew concerned that their children were losing their English identity. As a result, in 1620 they negotiated an agreement with the Virginia Company stockholders who years earlier had received from James I a charter to establish American colonies. In return for the use of a ship and some initial provisions, they agreed to share seven years of profits from the settlement with their investors.

Thus, in September 1620, just over one hundred passengers boarded the *Mayflower* and sailed for America. After exploring the coastline looking for a settlement site, they selected a location just north of Cape Cod, on a piece of land that Virginia's John Smith had previously named Plymouth. Because this site lay beyond the territory of Virginia, and they therefore had no legal basis for settling there, before leaving the ship forty-one adult males signed the Mayflower Compact. This contract was a simple statement that announced their allegiance to the king and a willingness to abide by rules decided upon by a majority of the adult males. Because they were religious wanderers who had traveled from Scrooby, England to Leyden, Holland to Plymouth, America, the settlers of Plymouth referred to themselves as "Pilgrims."

The Pilgrims stepped ashore just a few days before Christmas 1620, a dubious time of the year to establish a colony. Hit hard by disease and lack of provisions, only half of the original settlers survived the first winter. Unlike the Jamestown colonists, however, they did not squander their time looking for gold. Instead, as soon as spring arrived, they began cultivating their lands. Local natives, including Squanto and Samoset, befriended them, teaching them how to gather seafood and grow corn, and helping them to forge an alliance with Massasoit, the chief of the nearby Wampanoags. After reaping an abundant first harvest, in October 1621, they celebrated by inviting their Indian neighbors to a Thanksgiving festival.

Although stories of the Pilgrims and the establishment of Plymouth Colony are well known today, in the 17th century Plymouth Colony had only a modest impact on the colonial history of North America. Between its origins in 1621 and its merger with other territories in 1691 to form the Province of Massachusetts Bay, Plymouth Colony consisted of a small plantation that housed a tiny population of largely impoverished settlers. The Puritans largely responsible for shaping New England society were not this small band of Separatist Puritans who settled in Plymouth, but rather the more wealthy and plentiful non-separatist Puritans who began to arrive in Massachusetts about a decade after the coming of the Pilgrims.

REFORM OR PERISH: ENGLAND'S RELIGIOUS CRISIS & THE SETTLEMENT OF MASSACHUSETTS BAY

When James I died in 1625, his son Charles became the England monarch. English Puritans never liked James I, even though he gave them one of their demands – the publication of an English translation of the Bible (*The King James Version*, published 1611). While Puritans disliked James, they distrusted Charles I even more, and correctly recognized that Charles also distrusted them. Alarmed when Charles married Henrietta Maria, a devout Catholic and daughter of the king of France, the Puritans disliked Charles's domestic, diplomatic, and religious policies – including his support for those who taught a doctrine of salvation by faith coupled with good works, and his opposition to preaching on predestination.

When a depression hit England in the 1620s, many Puritans interpreted this as the beginning of God's wrath upon England for the corruption that allegedly was rampant in the Church of England. To these Puritans, intervention in some form was necessary to save the church and the nation from impending doom. When Charles had a dispute with Parliament in 1629, and dismissed it (for the next eleven years, Parliament would not meet), no entity existed to challenge the policies of a king who, at least from a Puritan perspective, was intent on bringing divine judgment on the land.

PAUSE-REFLECT-THINK

If you were an English Puritan in the late 1620s, what would you be willing to do to save your church and nation from experiencing the impending wrath of God?

If your idea is to escape England before it was condemned to hell, then you would have been a part of the minority of Puritans who felt it was their duty to condemn and leave the church. This position, while appropriate for Separatists, was rejected by most Puritans who felt called on to reform, not flee, the church. If your idea is to kill the king as a means to bring about reform, you would have been several decades ahead of your time. In the 1640s, Parliament with the support of many Puritans would go to war against the king, and in 1649, execute him. In 1629, however, this extreme option did not seem a godly response for Puritan leaders like John Winthrop. For Winthrop and the other leaders of Massachusetts Bay Company, a third option was suggested.

Like the Pilgrims who settled Plymouth Colony in 1620, the Puritans who would join the Massachusetts Bay Colony believed in Calvinistic doctrines (TULIP) and disliked the Church of England's government, theology, and lack of discipline. Unlike the Separatists, however, these Puritans believed that the Church of England was still God's church and could be purified.

When political circumstances in England frustrated their attempts at reform, these Puritan leaders led by John Winthrop concocted a scheme to buy out shares of stockholders who had secured from King Charles a land charter in North America similar to those previously granted by James I to stockholders of the original Virginia and Plymouth colonies. Unlike the investors in these earlier company colonies, however, the Puritan stockowners of the newly acquired Massachusetts Bay Company proposed to move en mass to America along with thousands of other like-minded Puritans that they would recruit to move with them.

Massachusetts Bay Company, at least on paper, would be a commercial company colony. To the Puritan investors who purchased it, however, it also would become a model "Christian Commonwealth" that would carry the Church of England with it to New England. When in New England, far away from the king's eyes, the people of Massachusetts Bay could govern the colony according to biblical principles. Because Puritans believed that the nature of God was to punish sin and reward obedience, these non-separating Puritans aspired to save their church and nation from impending calamity by setting an example for Old England to imitate. When God showered blessings upon New England (which the Puritans expected, assuming they remained obedient), the Puritans hoped that even the unregenerate king would acknowledge the error of his ways and bring godly reform to the church.

Perhaps this idea was naive, but at least to devout non-separating Puritans, it seemed to be a better Christian solution than doing nothing, separating, or killing the king, all of which would leave the nation in ruin. Thus, in 1630 about one thousand non-separating Puritans risked their lives and the lives of their children by coming to America with the hope of reforming the Church of England. The original fleet of seventeen ships led by Winthrop soon would be followed by scores of other ships carrying thousands of additional passengers, most of whom in the beginning were committed to the Puritan mission, but over time included more and more English subjects who simply aspired to make better lives for themselves and their families in the New World. Establishing Boston as the company headquarters and capital, the settlers quickly fanned out around this hub, dotting the region with small towns, each of which established a church and chose its own minister.

Creating a colony with such a lofty objective was not easy. Maintaining it was even harder. The seriousness of their mission encouraged them to punish moral laxity, expect hard work from everyone, and avoid all extravagance. They permitted social merriments, but refused to celebrate Christmas, Easter, and Maypole dancing because of their pagan origins. They allowed the drinking of intoxicants, but only in moderation, condemning drunkenness.

They considered sex within marriage as a gift from God to be enjoyed, not simply for the purposes of procreation. Similarly, they treated pre-marital sex with leniency and even permitted divorces for those whose spouses were impotent, too long absent, or cruel, but they punished severely adulterous and homosexual relationships.

They viewed their Native American neighbors as cultural (but not racial) inferiors, believing that they were descendants from one of the biblical Ten Lost Tribes of Israel whose original white skin had been darkened naturally by the sun and degenerate customs. This interpretation encouraged Puritan missionaries like John Eliot to translate the Bible into Algonquin language and to seek Christian converts among the natives.

Although the Puritans were not the "puritanical prigs" that historians a century ago portrayed them to be, they expected the inhabitants of Massachusetts Bay to live sober and godly lives, and those who deviated from these norms were greeted with considerable displeasure.

To ensure the success of their mission, most residents of the colony favored a close church and state relationship, although Massachusetts Bay ministers were not eligible for political office. Moreover, because Puritans considered marriage to be a civil union and not a religious sacrament, ministers also could not perform marriages. However, ministers carried great respect, and if they so willed, could influence the outcomes of colony elections.

The elected officials taxed the people to support churches, insisted that each town establish schools to teach children (girls included) to read the Bible, enforced laws demanding correct belief and compulsory church attendance, and granted only adult men who were recognized as full church members the right to vote in elections. In Massachusetts Bay, unlike in Old England, full church membership was not granted until the individuals requesting membership described their religious conversion experiences, and a majority of the congregation affirmed that the candidates were likely to be among those God predestined for salvation.

Although to modern eyes limiting voting rights to male church members who experienced religious conversions appears regressive, the decision to allow this actually was a democratic reform because according to the company charter, originally only the eight major stockholders had legal authority to establish colony laws. Nonetheless, as later settlers less committed to Winthrop's dream arrived in Massachusetts, tensions increased between the "saints" (meaning church members in good standing) who ruled the colony and the larger population.

Disagreements between church members, ministers, and civil magistrates were inevitable. In 1635, Thomas Hooker, a minister of the church in Newtown (later named Cambridge), voiced objections to the practice of granting voting rights to men only after an interrogation of their religious beliefs and conversion experiences. When this challenge was rebuked by John Cotton, an influential pastor in Boston, Hooker moved with about one hundred congregants to

Hartford, which at that time was wilderness territory more than a hundred miles to the west. Several years later, the people of Hartford, along with people in other western towns settled by other former Massachusetts Bay colonists, established an independent colony of Connecticut by adopting the Fundamental Orders of Connecticut, a constitution that granted all free men the right to participate in the election of magistrates.

During the early years of settlement, most Massachusetts Bay colonists supported the close alliance between church and state. One who did not, however, was Roger Williams.

TROUBLES IN ZION: THE CASE OF ROGER WILLIAMS

Roger and Mary Williams arrived in Boston from England in early 1631, less than one year after the original Massachusetts Bay settlers arrived with Winthrop. Williams was an Anglican minister who became attracted to Puritan ideas while in school at Cambridge, England. Williams had studied under Sir Edward Coke, one of the most famous intellectuals of the time. Coke was a strong proponent of individual and religious freedom who insisted, "a man's house is his castle," meaning that a person must be protected from intrusion by the government in his own house. As Chief Justice of the King's Bench, Coke promoted the concept of an English common law that applied equally to every person, rights that even kings could not alter by decree. When Coke argued against the concept of "divine right" rule – the notion that kings received their authority directly from God and therefore were not subject to any earthly authority – James I banished him to the Tower of London. Roger Williams deeply respected Coke, embraced his legal teachings, and imitated his determination to live a life consistent with one's convictions.

When Williams arrived in America, his reputation as a Puritan pastor led the leaders of the Boston church to invite him to be their teaching minister. However, Williams surprised and disappointed the elders of the Boston church by refusing their offer, stating that this church was insufficiently committed to God for him to have fellowship with it. He further antagonized Massachusetts authorities by publicly asserting that the Church of England must separate itself from civic government in order to fulfill the true tenets of Christianity.

After finding the church in Salem more in tune with his pious standards, Williams associated himself with that church and used its pulpit to proclaim a controversial message that included a call for the separation of church from state interference, and condemnation of practices that allowed the

King to deed land to companies and individuals without first purchasing it from the Native Americans.

On the topic of forcing religion on the natives or any other person, Williams boldly declared, "Forced Worship Stinks in God's Nostrils." As a well-respected scholar, Williams's words swayed people outside of his congregation, a situation quickly noticed by Governor Winthrop and other Puritans committed to their holy errand.

Because Williams's message included a call to limit the government and even the rule of the King, colonial leaders felt threatened, not only because Williams wanted to limit their range of local authority, but also because his words could provoke the King to remove their charter and take over the colony as James had done in Virginia only a decade earlier. Both the elected officials and ministers of Massachusetts Bay (equally powerful entities, although at this time ministers were not eligible to run for political office) urged Williams to cease this line of preaching, but he enthusiastically continued his crusade and refused to back down.

In July 1635, the General Court in Boston brought charges against Williams for proclaiming "diverse dangerous opinions." Interestingly, the indictment did not include a complaint against Williams's comments regarding the right of the King to disperse Indian lands, suggesting that by this date, Williams had largely satisfied his critics on this issue. The civic officials, however, charged Williams with disturbing the peace with his religious teachings. Some of the complaints concerned less profound issues, such as whether one should say a prayer before or after a meal. More central to the case, however, was Williams's opinion regarding a more fundamental question: to what degree should the state enforce the first four of the Ten Commandments?

Actually, there are multiple ways to create ten divine commands from the words contained in the Bible, but according to the 17th century count used by the Puritans, the four commandments in question were:

- thou shall have no other gods;
- thou shall not make any graven images;
- thou shall not take the name of the Lord in vain;
- thou shall remember the Sabbath and keep it holy.

These particular commandments, as well as the next one, "honor thy father and mother," have little to do with ethics and morality. To a greater degree than later commandments in the Decalogue (i.e., thou shall not kill, thou shall not steal, thou shall not commit adultery, etc.), the early commandments were largely theological ones that required interpretation to be understood and enforced. What entity should make these interpretations, and how should these rules be enforced? To these questions, Winthrop and Williams provided different answers.

Although a number of ministers supported Williams, the court only allowed those in opposition to speak and bring charges. Williams, who had a reputation as a powerful debater, answered every charge and refused to compromise on his primary issue: that the civic government should be separate from and not force any religious beliefs on its population.

In the end, the power and threats of the court even turned Williams's own (Salem) church against him. Only one minister failed to approve the sentence rendered against him. On October 9, 1635, Williams stood and heard the verdict:

> Whereas Mr. Roger Williams, one of the elders:of the church of Salem, hath broached and divulged diverse new and dangerous opinions, against the authority of magistrates…, and yet maintaineth the same without retraction, it is therefore ordered, that the said Mr. Williams shall depart out of this jurisdiction within six weeks.

POSTLUDE
DIVERSIFYING THE NEW ENGLAND WAY

Removing Roger Williams from Massachusetts did not end the debate over the appropriate balance between individual personal liberties and the right of a community to exert its preferences upon its members. Rather, it was simply the first skirmish in a war that is still being fought today.

One immediate consequence of the General Court's decision was that it led to the founding of Providence and the colony of Rhode Island, a town and colony that expressed equally ambitious but vastly different visions than did Massachusetts Bay.

Following his banishment from Massachusetts Bay, Williams spent the winter near the head of Narragansett Bay under the protection of the Wampanoags, and in spring 1636, purchased some land from Narragansett chiefs, and along with a dozen friends settled Providence, so named because they believed that God had brought them there.

While in Providence, Williams encountered some men and women who rejected the practice of infant baptism, a custom accepted by Catholics, Lutherans, Anglicans, and Calvinists alike. Persuaded by their scriptural arguments in favor of adult baptism, Williams had himself re-baptized, and gathered with this small group in worship, thus forming the first Baptist church in America. Within a few months, however, Williams broke fellowship with this church when he concluded that the church had become so corrupted that no human could claim God's authority to gather a community of true believers until Christ came again to announce this authority. Once again, following the dictates of his conscience, Williams left this church and became a "seeker." Although he remained a deeply spiritual person, Williams never again joined a church. His spiritual journey led him to espouse not only religious freedom, but also the individual freedom of conscience.

Williams wanted Providence to be a sanctuary for those like himself who were "distressed of conscience." In Massachusetts Bay, Winthrop made a distinction between natural liberty, which was the freedom to choose evil, and true liberty, which was the freedom to do "that only which is good," and "to quietly and cheerfully submit unto that Authority which is set over you." Winthrop, thus, supported a form of liberty, but it was the freedom to choose one way – God's way. Williams rejected this distinction, insisting that individual conscience must be respected. As a result, the civil compact that created Providence imposed no religious test for voting, offered no support for religion, and did not require compulsory church attendance – a choice that carried financial repercussions because at that time fines collected from those not attending church brought revenues to most government entities across England and New England alike.

As Providence grew, and along with it the neighboring towns of Portsmouth and Newport, legal battles over land rights propelled Williams to return to England to secure a charter for the land. In 1644, he returned with a charter approved by Parliament for the Colony of Rhode Island. In Rhode Island, individuals could practice any religion they wanted or no religion at all. To the Puritans of Massachusetts Bay, however, Rhode Island quickly developed the reputation of being the sewer of New England, the place where all the human waste ended up.

Among the Massachusetts Bay outcasts who would come to Rhode Island was Anne Hutchinson. A pious Puritan from a wealthy family with a brilliant mind to match her independent spirit, Hutchinson came to Massachusetts with her husband in 1634, purchased land next to the Winthrop estate, and soon began conducting religious meetings in her home after the traditional Sabbath services. Governor Winthrop and Hutchinson despised each other. Her vocal opposition to him contributed to Winthrop losing the 1636 election as governor of the colony, although Winthrop would regain the position the ensuing year. To Winthrop, Hutchinson was "more bold than a man, though in understanding and judgment, inferior to many women." Comments like these suggest that one reason Hutchinson posed such a threat to the ruling magistrates was that she was an outspoken women who dared to challenge social norms regarding the proper role of women in Puritan society.

Hutchinson's theological statements that got her into trouble were her complaints that a number of ministers in New England were preaching the same "covenant of works" (the idea that one could be saved by doing good works) that the Puritans had revolted against while in England. She even went so far as to assert that some of the Puritan ministers were not among those elected by God for salvation. When asked at her trial how she knew this, she claimed that the Holy Spirit communicated to her this truth. For her statements, she was convicted of holding two unorthodox views: antinomianism (the idea that there is no connection between being a Christian and being obedient to the laws of God), and enthusiasm (the belief that self-revelation supersedes the truth of Scripture). Hutchinson rejected both of these accusations, but like Williams, she was banished from Massachusetts by the General Court, and found sanctuary in Rhode Island, although later she moved to New Netherlands (New York) where she was killed when warring Indians attacked her village.

Because of her charisma and popularity, upon her banishment some who supported her teachings left with her. In the aftermath of her trial, Puritan clergy attempted to restrict even further the public religious activities of women. This retraction offended even more of her supporters, many of whom left Massachusetts in droves into towns that later would be incorporated into the future colony of New Hampshire.

INDIAN CONFLICTS & THE REEXAMINATION OF THE PURITAN MISSION

Puritan internal squabbles led to dissention, banishments, and new colonies, but not to massive death and destruction. The same cannot be said of their conflicts with Indian nations that occupied New England.

When the English arrived in New England, they shared the land with several indigenous nations in the region. Although geographical competitors, for much of the first half-century following the Pilgrim settlement of Plymouth, the English and the Native American peoples lived in peace on adjacent lands. The major exception to this rule was the brief Pequot War of 1636-37, which proved to be tragic for the Pequots when Massachusetts Bay and Connecticut put aside their differences and raised a militia that attacked and burned the Pequot village of Mystic, killing some three hundred people, mostly women and children. Ultimately, the Pequot suffered over four hundred war causalities and following the peace settlement, their survivors were divided among other Indian tribes or sold into slavery to the West Indies. Fortunately for the English, few Anglo lives were lost. One reason the English survived this war relatively unblemished was that Williams was able to persuade the Narragansett tribe to support the English in the war. After the Pequot War, New England again enjoyed a time of peace that lasted for about four decades.

This period of peace ended in 1675 when a feud between the Wampanoag chief Metacomet (known by the English as King Philip) and the descendants of the Plymouth Pilgrims deteriorated into a military confrontation that New Englanders would call King Philip's War. Angered by English intrusion onto his ancestral lands, Metacomet secured an alliance with the Narragansett and Nipmuck peoples and began raiding settlements in Connecticut and western Massachusetts. During the fighting and starvation that accompanied the war, about ten percent of the white male and thirty percent of the Native American populations in the area perished – staggering casualty rates rarely equaled in warfare. In addition to causing massive death and destruction, the war shattered whatever remaining goodwill existed between the two peoples. The Puritan vision of Christianized American Indians living harmoniously as peaceful neighbors was replaced with the sentiment that no Indian could be trusted, an attitude that made it easier for future generations to justify the elimination of native populations from New England.

King Philip's War also caused the Puritans to reexamine themselves and their mission. During its first half-century of settlement, the Puritan settlements in New England prospered in many ways. The average life expectancy in New England of those surviving infancy was about sixty-five years, more than ten years older than in Old England and twenty years older than those living in Virginia. Because migrants moved to New England in family units that included almost as many females as males, the natural born population grew more rapidly in New England than in the American south. By mid-century, New England's population stood at 23,000 (larger than even Virginia), and by 1680 it approached 70,000.

Longer life meant more working years and the potential for more money. Although New England did not produce exceedingly wealthy families, the lower poverty rates in the region meant that the average per capita wealth in New England exceeded that of England and most English colonies in America. New England's laws requiring schools in all towns did not educate everyone, but the literacy rates for both men and women were higher in New England than in most places in the world. Six years after the English arrived at Jamestown, they were living under martial law deemed necessary to maintain colony discipline and to prevent starvation. Six years after arrival in New England, the colonists established Harvard College to train colonial ministers. From these characterizations of New England life, one could say that the typical inhabitant of the region, comparatively speaking, was healthy, wealthy, and wise.

But for the Puritans who shared Winthrop's mission, prosperity had its drawbacks. From the beginning, Winthrop's religious values were challenged by those who were drawn to New England solely for commercial reasons. With the passing years, these aspiring Yankee capitalists were joined by increasing numbers of second and third generation New Englanders who also preferred pursuing earthly over heavenly treasures. For the pious remnant, the drop in church membership, especially among males, and the growing preoccupation with individual liberty or self-gain above community concerns were signs of spiritual declension. In 1662, Puritan clergy responded to the falling membership crisis by proposing the Half-Way Covenant – a compromise that permitted the children and grandchildren of full church members to the baptized even if their parents had not yet experienced a religious conversion. To many, this easier to obtain half-way church membership merely dramatized how far New England had fallen from the ideals of its founders.

PAUSE-REFLECT-THINK

If you were a New Englander in 1680 looking back upon the last half-century of Massachusetts Bay, would you have considered this colony to have been successful? With 21st century values, how would you answer this question?

If you answered this question in the affirmative, your measurements of success very likely were material ones. Indeed, by the numbers, New England could boast of many accomplishments.

However, if you defined success either as Williams did (the creation of a colony that granted liberty of conscience to all) or as Winthrop did (the creation of a colony that would inspire England to remake the Church of England into that of New England), then you probably would have concluded that the Puritan experiment was a failure because Massachusetts Bay neither embraced Williams's goal of offering liberty of conscience, nor succeeded in Winthrop's goal of transforming the Church of England.

THE WORLD OUTSIDE OF NEW ENGLAND

One reason that Old England did not pay greater attention to what was transpiring in New England was that during Massachusetts Bay's early years, political and religious tensions that had been simmering in England for decades erupted into all-out civil war. In 1642, Parliament and King Charles and their respective armies clashed. For seven years, a bloody civil war raged between the Cavaliers, who supported the king, and the Roundheads, mainly Puritans, who supported Parliament. In 1649, the Roundheads captured Charles I, and to the amazement of the world, beheaded their king and acknowledged Oliver Cromwell as England's Lord Protector.

Between 1652 and his death in 1658, Cromwell ruled as a as military dictator. For two years after Cromwell's death, his son Richard attempted to maintain authority, but the chaos and exhaustion of the previous decade had taken its toll. In 1660, Parliament voted to restore the monarchy by inviting Charles II to return from exile and claim the throne. The surviving judges that had been responsible for the beheading of Charles I were executed, and the body of Oliver Cromwell was exhumed and hanged in chains. In Restoration England, the Church of England again became the national church and required ministers to use the Book of Common Prayer in religious services. Nonconforming ministers were barred from holding civil or military office. Charles II favored granting Catholics the right to worship in public, but when Parliament balked at this plan, he prudently did not pursue it. Charles II proved to be a secret Catholic, as on his deathbed he converted to Catholicism.

The Restoration also resulted in a renewal of English interests in North American colonization. Before the outbreak of the English Civil War, six significant English colonies had been planted in the New World: two in the south (Virginia and

Maryland), and four in New England (Massachusetts Bay, Rhode Island, Connecticut, and New Hampshire). Separating these regions were settlements founded by the Dutch (New Netherlands – later New York), and the Swedes (New Sweden – later Delaware).

Between the Restoration (1660) and Charles's death (1685), Charles II attempted to enlarge England's empire by confronting the Netherlands, and establishing tighter control over the English colonies. While pursuing these goals, he created four new colonies: Carolina in the south and New York, New Jersey, and Pennsylvania in the mid-Atlantic region. Unlike Virginia and Massachusetts Bay, which were founded by private companies hoping to make quick profits, each of the new colonies was formed as a proprietary colony similar to Maryland. In each instance, Charles II gave loyal supporters both large land grants and wide authority to run them as they pleased.

In the south, Charles II awarded eight political supporters title to Carolina (a Latinate form of "Charles"). This grant included an immense tract of land stretching from Virginia to the Florida peninsula to the Pacific Ocean. Like the Lord Baltimores, the proprietors of Maryland, the Carolina proprietors also expected to extract great profits from land reserved for them and quitrents from the settlers that they would attract to the region. One of them, Sir Anthony Ashley

Cooper, had the philosopher John Locke draw up a constitution for the colony, which, if followed, would have a created a planned and well-ordered utopian society where landed aristocrats could govern benevolently with the consent of smaller landowners. In practice, the colony never came close to meeting these expectations as the northern and southern regions remained separated economically and culturally as well as geographically. Without deep harbors or navigable rivers, the northern land area attracted only poor backcountry farmers. Meanwhile, the southern region with its hub being Charles Town (later Charleston) achieved greater prosperity, largely by selling fur, hides, and Indian slaves to the English island colony of Barbados. Carolina remained politically fractured and unstable throughout the colonial era.

In the mid-Atlantic region, Charles II took advantage of Dutch weakness in the area by granting his brother James the Duke of York title to New Netherlands. In 1664, James sent a fleet that secured almost without opposition the surrender of the towns of New Amsterdam (renamed New York) and Fort Orange (renamed Albany). The colony that the Duke of York inherited was ethnically and religiously diverse, containing Dutch, French, German, Portuguese, English, Scandinavian, and African subjects who held Dutch Reform, Catholic, Lutheran, Quaker, and Jewish beliefs. James kept the bulk of his colony, which was named New

York, but parceled about five million acres of it to two friends, Sir John Berkeley and Sir George Carteret, who named their portion New Jersey.

James did not impose his Catholic religion on the people of New York and allowed some degree of religious toleration. However, he would not grant New Yorkers an elective assembly until 1683, and even then, rejected the Charter of Liberties passed by the assembly. James was never popular in New York, which like Carolina, remained unstable and embroiled in chronic political bickering throughout the remainder of the century.

The last land grant that Charles II awarded was Pennsylvania (meaning Penn's Woodlands). This colony was situated on a 45,000 square mile tract of land, which, unbeknownst to Charles, contained more minerals and fertile soil than any other American colony. In 1681, Charles II bestowed this land to William Penn Jr. after Penn inherited a claim on a loan that his father Sir William Penn had given to Charles's family.

Penn was an unlikely recipient of a land grant because he had only recently been released from prison for holding heretical views. As a member of the Society of Friends, a group more commonly known as Quakers, Penn requested from Charles II a tract of land that could be used as a sanctuary where Quakers could live without the threat of imprisonment or persecution. To pay off the family debt, Charles II agreed to Penn's request.

To most Anglicans, Catholics, Lutherans, and Puritans alike, the Quakers appeared strange. Convinced that God implanted within every soul an "Inner Light" – a speck of divinity – Quakers treated all people as worthy of divine respect. Consequently, they did not show partiality by bowing to alleged social superiors, and they allowed women as well as men to assume public roles as religious leaders. Being pacifists, they refused to go to war or serve in the military. They refused to take religious oaths required by English law. They lived simple lives; they wore non-ostentatious clothing and worshiped in simple meetinghouses, not fancy cathedrals. They had no paid clergy and during religious services, they followed no order of worship, but simply relied upon the Spirit to lead them. For these beliefs and practices, they were fined, whipped, and imprisoned.

While many English colonies did not live up to original expectations, the colony of Pennsylvania exceeded them. Unlike many proprietors, in 1682 Penn himself sailed to America, reimbursed the Indians for the land, and supervised the layout of its capital, appropriately named Philadelphia, the city of brotherly love. Thousands of settlers from northern Europe as well as England flocked to the colony because of its fertile land and its liberal government, which had created a representative assembly, guaranteed basic English liberties, and offered its inhabitants complete freedom of worship.

By the time of the death of Charles II, ten significant English colonies, some flourishing, others floundering, dotted the Atlantic seaboard. With each passing decade, these English colonies were growing more diverse – racially, religiously, and economically – and with this diversity came a clash of interests and competing visions and ambitions. Seeds of discontent watered by evolving desires for greater liberty were already being planted.

PROBING THE SOURCES: Competing Visions –Words from Winthrop & Williams

The first document containing excerpts from "A Model of Christian Charity" was written and delivered by John Winthrop while aboard the flagship *Arbella* en route to America. While it reads like a sermon, its author was the governor of Massachusetts Bay, not a minister. Directed to those who sailed with him on this "errand into the wilderness," Winthrop expressed the hopes and fears of the colony's organizers by describing how the colonists must act, socially and economically, for the colony to succeed.

The second document contains the Preface to *The Bloudy Tenet of Persecution* that Roger Williams wrote in 1643-44 while in England obtaining a charter for the colony of Rhode Island. This introduction outlined the arguments that Williams planned to articulate in his book.

The spelling in these 17th century sources has been modernized for easier reading.

Compare these competing visions of Christianity that were written by Puritans of different stripes. What arguments do you find to be persuasive and non-persuasive?

Document 1: Excerpts from "A Model of Christian Charity" by John Winthrop (1630)

> We are entered into covenant with [God] for this work, we have taken out a commission, the Lord hath given us leave to draw our own articles, we have professed to enterprise these actions, upon these and those ends, we have hereupon besought him of favor and blessing. Now if the Lord shall please to hear us, and bring us in peace to the place we desire, then hath he ratified this covenant and sealed our commission, [and] will expect a strict performance of the articles contained in

it. But if we shall neglect the observation of these articles, which are the ends we have propounded, and, dissembling with our God, shall fall to embrace this present world and prosecute our carnal intentions, seeking great things for ourselves and our posterity, the Lord will surely break out in wrath against us, be revenged of such a perjured people and make us know the price of the breach of such a covenant.

Now the only way to avoid this shipwreck, and to provide for our posterity, is to follow the counsel of Micah: to do justly, to love mercy, to walk humbly with our God. For this end, we must be knit together in this work as one man, we must entertain each other in brotherly affection, we must be willing to abridge ourselves of our superfluities, for the supply of others' necessities, we must uphold a familiar commerce together in all meekness, gentleness, patience and liberality; we must delight in each other, make others' conditions our own, rejoice together, mourn together, labor and suffer together, always having before our eyes our commission and community in the work, our community as members of the same body. So shall we keep the unity of the spirit in the bond of peace. The Lord will be our God, and delight to dwell among us as his own people, and will command a blessing upon us in all our ways, so that we shall see much more of his wisdom, power, goodness and truth, than formerly we have been acquainted with. We shall find that the God of Israel is among us, when ten of us shall be able to resist a thousand of our enemies; when he shall make us a praise and glory that men shall say of succeeding plantations: "the Lord make it like that of NEW ENGLAND." For we must consider that we shall be as a city upon a hill: The eyes of all people are upon us, so that if we shall deal falsely with our God in this work we have undertaken, and so cause him to withdraw his present help from us, we shall be made a story and a by-word through the world: we shall open the mouths of enemies to speak evil of the ways of God all professor for God's sake. We shall shame the faces of many of God's worthy servants, and cause their prayers to be turned into curses upon us, till we be consumed out of the good land whither we are going. ...

[B]eloved, there is now set before us life and good, death and evil, in that we are commanded this day to love the Lord our God, and to love one another, to walk in his ways and to keep his commandments and his ordinance and his laws, and the articles of our covenant with him, that we may live and be multiplied, and that the Lord our God may bless us in the land whither we go to possess it. But if our hearts shall turn away, so that we will not obey, but shall be seduced, and worship other Gods – our pleasures and profits – and serve *them*, it is propounded unto us this day, we shall surely perish out of the good land whither we pass over this vast sea to possess it:

Therefore let us choose life,
that we and our seed
may live by obeying His
voice and cleaving to Him,
for He is our life, and
our prosperity.

Document 2: Excerpts from the Preface of Roger Williams, *The Bloudy Tenet of Persecution* (1644)

> First, That the blood of so many hundred thousand souls of Protestants and Papists, spilt in the Wars of present and former Ages, for their respective Consciences, is not required nor accepted by Jesus Christ the Prince of Peace.
>
> Secondly, Pregnant Scriptures and Arguments are throughout the Work proposed against the Doctrine of persecution for cause of Conscience.
>
> Thirdly, Satisfactory Answers are given to Scriptures, and objections produced by Mr. Calvin, Beza, Mr. Cotton, and the Ministers of the New English Churches and others former and later, tending to prove the Doctrine of persecution for cause of Conscience.
>
> Fourthly, The Doctrine of persecution for cause of Conscience, is proved guilty of all the blood

of the Souls crying for vengeance under the Alter.

Fifthly, All Civil States with their Officers of justice in their respective constitutions and administrations are proved essentially Civil, and therefore not Judges, Governors or Defenders of the Spiritual or Christian state and Worship.

Sixthly, It is the will and command of God, that (since the coming of his Son the Lord Jesus) a permission of the most Paganish, Jewish, Turkish, or Antichristian consciences and worships, be granted to all men in all Nations and Countries: and they are only to be fought against with that Sword which is only (in Soul matters) able to conquer, to wit, the Sword of God's Spirit, the Word of God.

Seventhly, The state of the Land of Israel, the Kings and people thereof in Peace & War, is proved figurative and ceremonial, and no pattern nor president for any kingdom or civil state in the world to follow.

Eighthly, God requires not an uniformity of Religion to be enacted and enforced in any civil state; which enforced uniformity (sooner or later) is the greatest occasion of civil war, ravishing of conscience, persecution of Christ Jesus in his servants, and of the hypocrisy and destruction of millions of souls.

Ninthly, In holding an enforced uniformity of Religion in a civil state, we must necessarily disclaim our desires and hopes of the Jews conversion to Christ.

Tenthly, An enforced uniformity of Religion throughout a Nation or civil state, confounds the Civil and Religious, denies the principles of Christianity and civility, and that Jesus Christ is come in the Flesh.

Eleventhly, The permission of other consciences and worships that a state professes, only can (according to God) procure a firm and lasting peace, (good assurance being taken according to the wisdom of the civil state for uniformity of civil obedience from all sorts.)

Twelfthly, lastly, true civility and Christianity may both flourish in a state or Kingdom, notwithstanding the permission of diverse and contrary consciences, either of Jew or Gentile.

WHAT OTHERS SAY: Historians on the Legacy of Winthrop & Williams

Presented are excerpts from the works of three historians who have written about legacies of Winthrop and Williams. Which of these interpretations do you find to be the most and least compelling?

Document 1: Excerpts from Perry Miller, *Roger Williams: His Contribution to the American Tradition* (Bobbs-Merrill, 1953), pp. 254-57

[Williams] exerted little or no direction influence on theorists of the Revolution and the Constitution, who drew on quite different intellectual sources, yet as a figure and a reputation he was always there to remind Americans that no other conclusion than absolute religious freedom was feasible in this society....

Out of the exercise of his imagination he perceived that no man can be so sure of any formulation of eternal truth as to have a right to impose on the mind and spirit of other men. Williams further realized that he who does so impose truth on others is no longer concerned, in his heart of hearts, with the truth but only with the imposition.... [W]hat he stood for ... is the certainty that those who mistake their own assurances for divinely appointed missions, and so far forget the sanctity of others' persuasion as to try reducing them to conformity by physical means, commit in the face of the Divine a sin more outrageous than any of the statutory crimes....

By exposing false conceptions of purity and loyalty, he opened the way for a self-distrusting, undogmatic and yet firm resolution to seek for those goals in which alone the soul of man finds fulfillment.... Wherefore, he was able to contend through a long life for the essential freedom, saying constantly that if he perished, he perished, that eternity would pay for all. In the end, it may be that he is most valuable to us because he incarnates the fighter for ends who keeps always present to his consciousness a sense of his own fallibility, of his own insignificance, without ever for that reason giving over, without ever relaxing, the effort.

Document 2: Excerpts from Edmund Morgan, *The Puritan Dilemma: The Story of John Winthrop* (Harper Collins, 1958), pp. 130-32

Within a year or two [after banishment] Williams decided that the church must not include children simply on the basis of their parents' membership and abandoned the practice of infant baptism in the congregation he had gathered among the handful of the faithful who followed him to Providence. He had himself and all the other members rebaptized, but shortly began to question whether there could be a proper church at all until God raised up some new apostolic power. Finally he reached the position where he could not conscientiously have communion with anyone but his wife....

[Williams decided] that no church could attain purity in this world. He had effectively demonstrated the proposition to himself as he withdrew successively from the Church of England, from the churches of Massachusetts, and finally from everyone but his wife....

Winthrop was undoubtedly pained that Massachusetts had been unable to harness the zeal of so godly a man as Williams to the cause the colony was striving for. But he could take pride in the fact that the colony had not been split apart or lured into such an irresponsible pursuit of individual holiness as Williams advocated. The great majority of the population, even the great majority of the Salem church, kept their eyes on the goal that Winthrop had set them.

It was not a goal that any man would reach by himself, but a common goal which all must seek together, with church and state working side by side. It was a goal of godliness, and it needed godly men to reach it, but not those, like Williams, who pulled too hard and left the rest behind. If such wild ones could not be tamed, it was best to cut them loose, lest they overturn the whole enterprise.

Document 3: Excerpts from John M. Barry, *Roger Williams and the Creation of the American Soul: Church, State, and the Birth of Liberty* (Viking, 2012), pp. 1-6

The Massachusetts authorities and Williams would have it out over their great dispute, but they would not settle it, nor is it settled now. For their dispute defined for the first time two fault lines that have run continuously through four hundred years of American history....

The first...the proper relation between what man has made of God – the church – and the state. The second...the proper relation between a free individual and the state – the shape of liberty, the form American individualism would take....

The Bay's leaders, both lay and clergy, firmly believed that the state must enforce all of God's laws, and that to do so the state had to prevent error in religion....

Williams recognized that putting the state to that service required humans to interpret God's law.... [H]e believed that humans, being imperfect, would inevitably err in applying God's law. Hence, he concluded that a society built upon the principles that Massachusetts espoused could at best lead only to hypocrisy, for he believed that forced worship "stinks in God's nostrils." At worst, it would lead to a foul corruption not of the state, which was already corrupt, but of the church, as it befouled itself with the state's errors. His understandings were edging him toward a belief he would later call "Soul Libertie."....

It would be [Williams], not Thomas Jefferson, who first called for a "wall of separation" to describe the relationship of church and state which both he and Jefferson demanded. It would be he who created the first government in the world that built such a wall. And it would be he who first defined the word "liberty" in modern terms, and saw the relationship between a free individual and the state in a modern way.

LOOKING BACKWARD/LOOKING FORWARD: Viewing Themes Across Time & Place

A "Locating Themes across Time and Place" Exercise:

First, review this chapter for information on the monarchs and lord protectors of England from Henry VIII through Charles II. Associate each executive with a descriptor of his/her religious preferences. The descriptor can be either the name of a group (i.e., Catholic, Puritan, etc.) or a noun or adjective that captures the religious sentiment of the person (i.e., via media, comprehension, etc.).

Second, review this chapter for information on each of the aborted or successful English settlements in North America, and create a descriptor that connects that settlement with a religious preference. Finally, chronologically arrange your lists to create a timeline of monarchs, settlements, and religious preferences during the Tudor/Stuart periods.

A Project Based Learning Assignment: Diagraming Geographical Historical Connections

Gather with a group of students who completed the above exercise and compare your respective timelines. Following this discussion, create three circles, entitling them, respectively, Southern Colonies, Northern Colonies, and

Middle Colonies. Insert inside of the circles (a) the names of the colonies in each region, (b) the names of major individuals and events associated the region, and (c) three to five historical trends associated with the region. Search the internet for information on the creation of Venn diagrams.

Create a Venn diagram of three interconnecting circles, labeling the circles the Southern, Northern, and Middle Colonies. Examine the historical trends that you identified in the above activity (or create additional historic trends not previously identified) and place these historical trends into one of the seven areas of your Venn diagram depending upon whether the trend occurred in one region, two regions, or all three regions. Place your three circles and the Venn diagram you created on slides, and present to the class a 10-minute lecture that discusses English colonization in 17th century America.

SUGGESTED READINGS

Edmund Morgan has written short, lively biographies on each of the central characters in this chapter. Both are worth reading. See his *The Puritan Dilemma: The Story of John Winthrop* (Pearson, 2006) and *Roger Williams: The Church and State* (Norton, 2007). Other interpretative biographies pertinent to the themes of this chapter are John M. Barry, *Roger Williams and the Creation of the American Soul:*

Church, State, and the Birth of Liberty (Viking, 2012), and Edwin Gaustad, *Liberty of Conscience: Roger Williams in America* (Judson Press, 1999). For an introduction to another central figure in the history of Massachusetts Bay, see Timothy Hall, *Anne Hutchinson*: *Puritan Prophet* (Longman, 2010). To understand the essence and appeal of Puritanism, see Harry Stout, *The New England Soul: Preaching and Religious Culture in Colonial New England* (Oxford University Press, 2011) and Charles Cohen, *God's Caress: The Psychology of Puritan Religious Experience* (Oxford University Press, 1988). For two very different but interesting introductions to life in Virginia, see Ivor Hume, *The Virginia Adventure: Roanoke to James Towne* (University of Virginia Press, 1997) and Kathleen Brown, *Good Wives, Nasty Wenches, and Anxious Patriarchs: Gender, Race, and Power in Colonial Virginia* (University of North Carolina Press, 1996).

ONLINE RESOURCES

Historical Drawings
Arnoldo Arnoldi's Pictorial Map of the Americas, 1600
http://www.loc.gov/resource/g3290.ct001452/

John Smith's Pictorial Map of Virginia, 1624
http://www.loc.gov/item/99446115/

John Winthrop's Sketch of the Boston Area, 1633
http://etc.usf.edu/maps/pages/8500/8527/8527.htm

Illustrations

Portrait of John Winthrop
http://upload.wikimedia.org/wikipedia/commons/1/15/John_Winthrop_lithograph_004.JPG

Franklin Simmons Statue of Roger Williams
http://en.wikipedia.org/wiki/Roger_Williams_%28theologian%29#mediaviewer/File:Roger_Williams_statue_by_Franklin_Simmons.jpg

Maps

Land Grants to the London and Plymouth Companies, 1606
http://etc.usf.edu/maps/pages/5200/5272/5272.htm

17th Century New England
http://etc.usf.edu/maps/pages/7600/7698/7698.htm

The Middle Colonies in the 17th Century
http://etc.usf.edu/maps/pages/7600/7697/7697.htm

Colonial North America, 1650-1700

http://etc.usf.edu/maps/pages/5200/5274/5274.htm

North American Exploration and Settlement Before 1675

http://www.lib.utexas.edu/maps/united_states/exploration_before_1675.jpg

Quantitative Data

Colonial and Pre-federal Statistics – Z Series

http://www2.census.gov/prod2/statcomp/documents/CT1970p2-13.pdf

Chapter 4:
Awakening the Enlightened, November 8, 1739: George Whitefield, Benjamin Franklin & the Wars & Cultural Wars of the 18th Century

PRELUDE

On the eve of Halloween 1739, George Whitefield arrived in Lewes, Delaware. One week later, this twenty-four-year-old, confident, charismatic celebrity minister preached at Christ Church, Philadelphia. Already world-renowned for holding open-air revivals in Bristol and London before crowds of upwards of 50,000, Whitefield was too grand a show to be limited to a church house. Following the service, congregants urged him to move outdoors to a place that could accommodate larger crowds.

Two days later, on November 8, Whitefield preached extemporaneously from the courthouse steps to 6,000 people, approximately one-half of Philadelphia's population. His audience was wide-based, including well-to-do deists like Benjamin Franklin, and hundreds of curious African American laborers who found the theatrical performances of Whitefield to be both inspiring and entertaining.

This would be the first of many outdoor services Whitefield would preach in the region. Although his official assignment was to be the pastor for an Anglican parish in Savannah, Georgia, between this day and Christmas 1740, Whitefield delivered about 350 public sermons outside of Savannah, including 96 in Pennsylvania and 89 in New England. Boston and Philadelphia produced his largest crowds. Whitefield also preached in New York, a city with less interest in evangelical religion, where his largest crowd reached a mere 5,000 people, still nearly half of the population. In Philadelphia, in contrast, Whitefield once preached to 20,000 listeners, while at his farewell sermon in Boston, the newspapers estimated 23,000. Given that Boston's population at the time was only 13,000, crowds this large suggest that nearly half of those attending the event traveled by horse or foot from afar to hear the evangelist speak. Whitefield's appearances created events that look like modern-day Super Bowls. To use a 1960s analogy, Whitefield was the "Woodstock" of colonial America.

What made this charismatic preacher so popular, and what was the lasting significance of his tours of the American colonies? Neither of these questions has a simple and singular answer, but to provide the context necessary to consider possible explanations, let us first survey the state of the British American colonies during the decades leading up to Whitefield's arrival.

CLASHING EMPIRES: A GLORIOUS REVOLUTION & 4 WORLD WARS

Wars often carry multiple names. In the 20th century, historians named and numbered massive international conflicts as world wars (i.e., World War I, World War II). If this nomenclature had been followed during the century before the American Revolution, then another name for the American Revolution (1775-1783) would have been World War V, with the world wars preceding it being named:

World War IV (1756-1763) – Seven Years' War, or the French and Indian War

World War III (1739-1748) – War of Austrian Succession, or King George's War

World War II (1701-1714) – War of Spanish Succession, or Queen Anne's War

World War I (1689-1697) – Nine Years' War, or King Williams's War

In each of these world wars, England and France were on

opposing sides, as they would be again in the wars of the French Revolution (1793-1802) and the Napoleonic Wars (1803-1815).

The trigger to the first of these Anglo-French world wars, and thus indirectly the trigger to all seven of them, was the Revolution of 1688. This event, also called "The Glorious Revolution," was a pivotal yet bloodless English civil conflict that overthrew the Catholic King James II and replaced him with the Protestant monarchs William and Mary. The outcome of this Glorious Revolution set the stage for a clashing of empires that would cause lasting reverberations on both sides of the Atlantic.

James II ruled England for less than four years (1685-1688), but it was long enough for him to create sufficient enemies to take away his crown. As the second son of Charles I and Henrietta Maria, James II, formerly the Duke of York, took the throne on the death of his elder brother, Charles II. Charles II, who was known as the "Merry Monarch," had at least twelve children through various mistresses, but none of his children were legitimate and all were therefore ineligible for the throne. Hence, James II became king. Within months after his coronation, James II, a Catholic like his mother, became despised by large majorities at home and in the colonies for his policies and his religion.

In America, James II was disliked for some of the same reasons his brother Charles II was unpopular. In the second half of the 17th century, England began to commit itself, as did its European rivals, to an economic theory, "mercantilism," which defined national strength in terms of the amount of gold that could be acquired by selling more goods to other nations than were purchased from them. To achieve this "favorable balance of trade," England expected its colonies to provide the motherland with raw materials that could be manufactured into exportable finished and more expensive goods, to reduce the need for imports by growing for England the commodities it desired, to build and supply ships needed for trade, and to be a market for English-made goods.

To encourage the colonies to focus on these patriotic duties, first under the rule of Oliver Cromwell and later under Charles II, Parliament passed a series of Navigation Acts, which provided benefits to colonists who performed these tasks. While helpful in some ways, these acts prohibited the colonists from trading directly (buying or selling) with the Netherlands, France, and Spain, and imposed tariffs on foreign-produced goods, thus raising the prices colonists paid for these items.

As patriotic English men and women who wanted England to compete well against its rival empires in the international commercial game of mercantilism, some colonists accepted the wisdom of these acts, but this support was not universal. In the Chesapeake, planters pouted over England's regulation of its tobacco, while in New England and the middle colonies, many simply ignored the Navigation Acts by carrying on illegal trade with the Dutch. To enforce these acts regulating trade, or at least to prevent flagrant violations of them, Charles II sent customs officials to America. Additionally, he increased his authority over Massachusetts, first by making New Hampshire into a separate royal colony and later by revoking Massachusetts's charter and turning it into a royal colony.

Massachusetts disliked Charles II, but it would quickly grow to hate his successor even more. As monarch, James II combined Massachusetts with the other New England colonies as well as New York and New Jersey to create a single entity known as the Dominion of New England. The mission of the Dominion was to unify the colonies under a single governor, eliminate the legislative assemblies (which interfered with royal policies), and ensure greater compliance with the acts of trade. James II thus abolished the representative assemblies in these former colonies and appointed a single governor, Sir Edmund Andros, to administer the entire region. Andros ruled New England as if the colonists had lost all of their English rights upon arrival in America. He further offended many

New Englanders by demanding that Anglican services be conducted in Boston's Puritan churches, restricting the New England tradition of holding town meetings, and introducing quitrents as a means of raising revenues.

James II was equally despised at home. By and large, the nation mourned the death of his brother, Charles II, even though many did not appreciate Charles's alliances with the Catholic superpower France against the Protestant Netherlands, his numerous Catholic mistresses, or his deathbed conversion to Catholicism. James II, however, was not a closet Catholic. Like his mother Henrietta Maria, James II openly supported the Roman Church, and demonstrated this loyalty by appointing Catholics to important military and civic positions, issuing the Declaration of Indulgence (which granted religious toleration for multiple Christian traditions, including Catholicism), and removing the penal laws that enforced conformity in the Church of England. Like his father Charles I, James II also had no qualms about asserting his authority over Parliament, or sending it home when he disagreed with it.

When James became monarch, he had two daughters, Mary and Anne, both of whom were Protestant. In June 1688, however, James II announced the birth of James Edward, and assured the nation that his son would be raised as a Catholic. Fearful of a bitter religious war, members of Parliament invited James's eldest daughter Mary and her husband, William of Orange, the Protestant ruler of the Netherlands, to be co-monarchs. William and Mary accepted the offer, and in November entered England with their army. The coup was "glorious" because it was both successful and bloodless, as William and Mary allowed James II, his wife, and son to escape to France.

In America, news of this Glorious Revolution inspired an uprising that toppled Andros's regime. William and Mary allowed the collapse of the short-lived Dominion of New England and the reinstatement of most of the former separate colonies, although over time the English monarchs did make some changes, including the official joining of Massachusetts and Plymouth into a single royal colony of which the Crown had the authority to appoint its governor. They also required Massachusetts to tolerate Anglican worship, and to change voting eligibility requirements from adult male church members to adult male landowners.

Meanwhile, in New York, a wealthy German immigrant named Jacob Leisler took advantage of the fall of Andros by proclaiming to be the new head of government. The new monarchs did not support Leisler's uprising. In 1691, Leisler was hanged and quartered for treason, and for decades New York politics would be torn between pro- and anti-Leisler factions.

Further to the south, in Maryland the Glorious Revolution provoked another revolt against the officials who administered Lord Baltimore's colony. As in Massachusetts, William and Mary permitted the results of this coup by stripping the proprietor of his authority, and by allowing the Protestants who controlled the Maryland assembly to establish the Anglican Church as the colony's official religion. The Maryland assembly also took advantage of its freedom by passing laws that prohibited Catholics from voting, holding public office, or conducting public worship in the colony. In 1715, Maryland again would be designated a proprietary colony but only after the fifth Lord Baltimore converted to Anglicanism and announced his loyalty to the Church of England.

Just as the Glorious Revolution altered life in the colonies, the fleeing of the former English king to France also triggered an Anglo-French rivalry that would influence international relationships for more than a century. Rather immediately, this clash of empires contributed to the outbreak of the War of the League of Augsburg (or King Williams's War, 1688-97), a conflict that lasted nearly a decade but ended without an exchange in colonial territories. After a few years of peace, the War of Spanish Succession (or Queen Anne's War, 1701-14) again pitted England against France, which was allied with Catholic Spain. Following nearly a dozen more years of fighting, Great Britain (a nation-state formed by the 1707 union of England and Scotland) secured Nova Scotia, Newfoundland, and the Hudson Bay region from France.

The victorious peace did not eliminate Britain's fear of the powerful Franco-Spanish alliance, but dynastic concerns did impose a temporary peace between the rival empires. Shortly after the peace settlement, Queen Anne died without surviving offspring, and the British Crown was offered to her distant cousin George Hanover, a German ruler who was a descendent of a daughter of James I. As a German, not only was George I less interested in the expansion of Britain's American empire, but he also had good cause to focus his immediate attention on protecting his own claim to the throne. Meanwhile, a year after Anne's death, Louis XIV – the aging monarch of France – also died, and his five-year-old grandson, Louis XV, became the new king. After over two decades of nearly continuous warfare, both empires were happy, at least for a while, to assume more defensive than offensive postures.

Under George I and his successor George II, Britain looked for ways to bolster its southern frontier against potential threats from French Catholics in Louisiana and Spanish Catholics in Florida. General James Oglethorpe proposed to George II an innovative solution that promised to solve a number of Britain's problems with one swoop. His proposal was to create a southern buffer colony that would protect South Carolina from future invasions, and populate the new colony by releasing and transporting British convicts imprisoned for debt. This plan, thus, would create a garrison that would guard the colonial borders, give Britain's "worthy poor" a second chance at life, and reduce the soaring budget of Britain's prison system.

In 1732, George II accepted Oglethorpe's plan, and Georgia – Britain's thirteenth colony – was established. Georgia's original charter differed from all of the other British colonies. The colony initially was to be run by trustees like Oglethorpe who could raise money, distribute lands, and levy taxes, but could not themselves profit from the venture. A humanitarian as well as a military venture, governed by philanthropists not profit seekers, Georgia was intended to be a paternalistic society that not only provided Britain's down-and-outers with small tracts of land, but also protected them from temptations that could bring about their demise. For example, the trustees did not allow the colonists to own more than 500 acres, sell their lands, drink liquor, hold slaves, or legislate with elected assemblies. To ensure that the colonists did not aid potential Catholic invaders, the trustees also prohibited Catholic worship in the colony. Unsurprisingly, few debtors took advantage of this opportunity, and soon the idealistic policies of the trustees gave way. Ultimately,

Georgia would develop agricultural patterns similar to the other southern colonies.

In the 1740s and again in the 1750s, the period of peace ended as two more global conflicts pitted Britain against its two Catholic rivals. As in all of the world conflicts of this century, the wars would be fought in both European and American theaters. For much of the late 17th and 18th centuries, the major European empires, each wanting to dominate trade and win the game of mercantilism, became entrenched in hot and cold wars that impacted both the territorial status and patterns of settlement and life in the American colonies.

AMERICA IN TRANSITION: SAINTS TO SELLERS, SERVANTS TO SLAVES

The latter decades of the 17th century were difficult years for the descendants of the Puritans who had come to New England with high hopes just three generations earlier. After a lengthy period of largely peaceful relations with the Native Americans, in 1676 King Philip's War brought proportionally greater devastation and death to the region than would be experienced in any subsequent war fought in North America. That same year a tragic fire engulfed Boston, destroying large portions of the city. In 1679, Charles II forced the establishment of an Anglican Church in Boston, and five years later revoked the Massachusetts Bay charter. In the future, if godly reform were to take place in the colony, it would have to be the work of the church alone, not the originally envisioned godly co-partnership between the Puritan church and state. In 1687, the new Catholic King James II added insult to injury by creating the despised Dominion of New England. Although the Glorious Revolution did oust this "Catholic tyrant," in 1691 the new monarchs William and Mary reestablished Massachusetts as a royal colony, and altered voting requirements in ways that gave political influence to the wealthy, not to the spiritual.

PAUSE-REFLECT-THINK

What would second or third generation Puritans who remained committed to Winthrop's original mission think about what was transpiring in New England during the latter decades of the 17th century? How might a Puritan of this mindset explain why these events were occurring?

Sermons and publications of late 17th century Puritan ministers suggest that Puritans in this period were obsessed with two ideas: (1) It was God's nature to express displeasure with wickedness by chastising the unfaithful, and (2) Public morality and piety in New England were in decline. Because of these assumptions, many Puritans read natural experiences such as fires and floods, and human-induced calamities such as wars and political retributions as signs of divine judgments. To these thinkers, the events of the 1670s and 1680s did not bode well for the spiritual climate of the region or for the future of New England.

Works by the influential Puritan minister Reverend Increase Mather, and his equally renowned son, Reverend Cotton Mather, bemoaned the waning of the Holy Spirit from New England. In his book *An Earnest Exhortation to the Inhabitants of New-England to Harken to the Voice of God* (1676), Increase Mather issued the warning that the outbreak of King Philip's War was God's punishment on the people of New England for backsliding. A few years later Mather expressed concerns about the use of occult practices in the region, warning in his *An Essay for the Recording of Illustrious Providences* (1684) that it was better to die "than to go to the Devil for health." His son Cotton Mather echoed similar concerns in his 1689 publication *Memorable Providences Relating to Witchcraft and Possessions*, asserting in the introduction to the volume: "Go tell Mankind, that there are Devils and Witches…New-Engl[and] has had Examples of their Existence and Operation; and that not only [in] the Wigwams of Indians…but the House of Christians…have undergone the Annoyance of Evil spirits."

In the midst of these concerns with religious declension and political turbulence, in early 1692 in the town of Salem, adolescent daughters of Reverend Samuel Parris showed hysterical behavior and accused certain individuals of bewitching them. As the number of girls with symptoms increased, the local magistrates demanded action. In response, the colony governor appointed a special court to try the cases against the accused witches, many of whom had achieved considerable economic power, often through their husbands' deaths. Also among the accused were non-Anglo servants, and women disinclined to remarry.

These characteristics of the accused suggest that the Salem Witch trials were about more than a community's belief in (and lack of toleration for) occult practices. The trials were also a crackdown on women who threatened male authority by not observing the gender roles expected of them. Before the court was adjourned, more than 150 had been accused of witchcraft, one man was crushed to death while being tortured to secure a confession, and nineteen had been hanged. Years later, Ann Putnam appeared before her congregation to confess that she was

> an instrument for the accusing of several persons of a grievous crime, whereby their lives were taken away from them, whom now I

> have just grounds and good reason to believe they were innocent persons; and that it was a great delusion of Satan that deceived me in that sad time, whereby I justly fear I have been instrumental, with others, though ignorantly and unwittingly, to bring upon myself and this land the guilt of innocent blood . . . .

The tragedy at Salem in 1692 did not mark the end of an era, but it did illustrate a transition that was taking place in several regions of America around the turn of the century. In a book on colonial Connecticut titled *From Puritan to Yankee: Character and the Social Order in Connecticut, 1690-1765*, in the book title itself, Richard Bushman succinctly captures a cultural shift that was occurring simultaneously in a number of English colonies. The title of Frederick Tolles's work on colonial Pennsylvania, *Meeting House and Counting House: The Quaker Merchants of Colonial Philadelphia, 1682-1763*, also encapsulates a similar transition that was occurring in the middle colonies.

During these decades, rising economic ambitions gradually altered the structure of colonies earlier created as religiously focused, community-centered societies, converting them into more commercially successful and secular societies that allowed individuals to pursue their own self-interests.

The descriptive phrases from Puritan to Yankee (the word here refers to a merchant-on-the-make, a capitalist) and from Meeting House (church) to Counting House (bank) suggest the emergence of consumer culture centered more on sellers than saints. The more market driven world of the middle and northern colonies of the 18th century enlarged the bounds of economic liberty even as it inspired greater resistance to established religious authority.

Meanwhile, the late 17th and early18^{th} century also brought profound economic changes in the south. Southern planters depended largely on cash crops – tobacco in the Chesapeake and rice and indigo in the Carolinas and Georgia – for their livelihood. Because the cultivation of these crops required a large labor supply, planters sought workers wherever they could find them, first recruiting indentured servants from England, and later purchasing African slaves from Portuguese and Dutch slave traders. 17th Century slavery existed in the Chesapeake, but it was exceedingly rare. Before 1660, not more than one in twenty laborers working the tobacco plantations in the Chesapeake was an African slave.

The subtle shift from indentured servitude toward race-based slavery began to appear in the 1660s when the Virginia House of Burgesses enacted laws that supported the institution of chattel slavery. Because slavery had not been practiced in England for centuries, the early Virginia colonists knew little about the legalities of servitude for life, although they were aware that English settlers in Barbados had passed legislation certifying that Indian and African slaves purchased on the island were to be enslaved for life. In the 1660s, the Virginians adopted this model by declaring that the offspring of enslaved women became the property of the master. This action had enormous and nefarious consequences in that it instantaneously made profitable rape and forced breeding.

About this same time in England, Charles II chartered what soon came to be known as the Royal African Company. Although originally created to exploit the gold fields along Africa's west coast, this business partnership between the Crown and London merchants soon began trading in human cargo as well as gold. During the 1670s and 1680s, the Royal African Company exported around 5,000 slaves a year, the majority of whom were sold in the Caribbean, but some to planters in the southern colonies.

Given the growing demand for slave laborers in the region, these numbers would have been even higher were it not for high prices the company was able to charge because of its monopoly over trade with Africa. Following the Glorious Revolution, both southern planters and English merchants opposed the exclusive deal given to the Royal African Company. Around the turn of the century, Parliament yielded to this pressure by opening slave trade to any merchant willing to pay a ten percent duty to the Royal African Company. With the breaking of the monopoly, the prices of slaves dropped, and soon 20,000 Africans were being sold against their wills into the English colonies every year.

Between 1700 and the end of the British slave trade in the mid-19th century, as many as twenty million Africans were captured in West and Central Africa and sold at ports around the world, over ten million of whom arrived as slaves in the Americas. Those sold into slavery actually were among the more fortunate, because millions of others (approximately fifteen percent of the total) either died in chains crammed into narrow spaces (16 inches wide, 30 inches tall) aboard filthy, windowless ships during their "middle passage" to America, or perished on a lonely shore far from home before the day of their sale.

In the Carolinas, Indian slavery as well as African slavery was a big business, as colonial traders purchased slaves from Indian allies and then exported them to other colonies or to the Caribbean. The profitability of this trade motivated raids into Spanish Florida that resulted in a rapid depopulation of Indians in the region. In retaliation for these atrocities, in 1715 the Yamasee Indians took to the offensive, striking English settlements across South Carolina and threatening Charles Town. This short-lived Yamasee War resulted in massive destruction and loss of life, but it also inspired new diplomatic alliances among the warring Indians that ended the lucrative Carolina Indian slave trade. After 1715, South Carolina rice planters would rely less on forced Indian labor and more on the importation of African slave labor.

THE FACTS OF LIFE: MIGRATION, SEX, & MARRIAGE

Population increase or decrease depends on four things: in-flow, out-flow, procreation, and death. During the colonial period, the relative significance of each of these factors varied by era and the region of settlement.

In the 17th century, the total non-indigenous population of the English colonies in North America never exceeded a quarter of a million, with the majority of the colonists living in New England or in the Chesapeake. The population profile and growth factors of these regions varied dramatically.

In New England, growth depended little on immigration, as approximately as many settlers arrived during its first decade of settlement as arrived during the remainder of the 17th century. Because of the approximately equal ratio of men to women, New England birth rates were high. Early marriages also contributed to high birth rates, as most New England women married before age 22 (about three years earlier than women in England did) and had their first child by age 23.

With sufficient food and the relative absence of disease, New England's death rates were remarkably low. For men and women who lived into adulthood, New England life expectancies in the 17th century were 69 years for men and 62 years for women. These averages were twelve to seventeen years longer than in Old England, and at least among men, closer to 21st century United States norms than 17th century European ones. Because one in seven colonial women died during her childbearing years giving birth, women at age 20 had shorter life expectancies than men, but longer life expectancies than men at age 50. Owing to these high fertility and low mortality rates, as early as the mid-17th century, most New Englanders were born in America, not in England.

A very different pattern emerged the early southern colonies. Owing to famine, war, and disease – largely caused by insufficient provisions, hostilities with the Indians, and an inhospitable geography – early Virginia experienced high death and ex-migration rates. In its early years the only reason Virginia survived was because its sponsors kept recruiting and sending warm bodies to keep the colony alive. Even a half century later, most Virginians fortunate to survive to adulthood died before age 50.

Moreover, although the early eight-to-one male to female ratio improved over time to a mere three to one male dominance, throughout the 17th century Virginia's unbalanced sex ratio slowed the colony's birth rates. Fertility rates would have been even lower were it not for the fact that the typical southern woman was married by age 20. On the positive side, the scarcity of women in Virginia actually presented 17th century southern women with more economic freedom and social mobility than 17th century New England women or future 18th and 19th century southern women.

As slavery became codified into law, forced breeding practices resulted in more African births, and by 1700 more slaves were being conceived in the Chesapeake than imported from Africa. Yet outside the Chesapeake in the swampy rice plantations of South Carolina, death rates and slave importation rates remained high. Unlike in the Chesapeake region, in South Carolina immigration remained the primary source of population growth throughout the colonial period.

At 1680, almost a century after Sir Walter Raleigh attempted to plant an English colony in America, the population of the English colonies totaled about 150,000, with about eight in ten descending from England, one in twenty from Wales, one in twenty from Scotland, one in twenty from Africa, and one in twenty from other world regions. Twenty years later at the turn of the 18th century, the population stood at 250,000, still largely English, but now with a ten percent and growing African minority. During the final decades of the 17th century, some 1,500 French Huguenots also made their way to the English colonies after Louis XIV revoked the Edict of Nantes, which had previously granted religious freedom to French Protestants. Despite these changes, at the turn of the 18th century British America was largely as Raleigh had predicted it to be: a collection of little Englands.

Between 1700 and 1763, the population of British America soared from 250,000 to 1,600,000. With fewer than one in ten adult women being unmarried, and most of the remaining nine in ten giving birth to five to eight children, in the 18th century British America's birth rate was double that of Britain, and triple current United States rates. These high birth rates, coupled with a doubling of the 17th century immigration rates, resulted in one of the most rapidly exploding population booms in world history.

Complementing this robust quantitative change were profound ethnic and social changes. Nearly half of all immigrants coming to America during these years were Africans, a plurality of whom were sold as slaves in the southernmost colonies of South Carolina and Georgia. By the 1740s, on the average, an additional one thousand slaves arrived every month. With this influx plus the rapidly growing numbers of Chesapeake-born Africans, by the 1760s nearly one in five people in the English colonies was an enslaved African.

During the first quarter of the 18th century, the flow of English immigrants, on average, trickled to no more than 100 new arrivals per year, but offsetting this slowdown in English migration were increasing numbers of French, German, Swiss, Scottish, and Irish immigrants who were fleeing religious persecution in their homelands. German pietistic groups immigrated in great numbers, particularly to Pennsylvania, where they made up more than one-third of its population. Meanwhile, thousands of Scots-Irish (Scottish Presbyterians who had settled in Ireland the previous century) scattered into the English colonies after the British government prohibited Presbyterianism in northern Ireland. Scottish Highlanders – including many Roman Catholics who were persecuted under George I and George II for refusing to recognize the legitimacy of the Hanoverian dynasty – also flocked to the colonies, as did growing numbers of Irish Catholics. By 1763, the ethnic complexion of the thirteen English colonies was significantly more diverse than it was at the beginning of the century.

The more ethnically diverse population was also becoming more economically diversified. At the beginning of the century, a huge gap separated the material quality of life of Anglos and Africans, but within Anglos, the gap between the richer and poorer was minimal. Yet, during the course of the 18th century, even as the proportion of the enslaved population doubled, the wealth of merchants grew at a more rapid pace than that of artisans and laborers.

Moreover, as the population grew, the size of inheritable land diminished, making it more difficult for individuals to launch successful careers. Even in the south, where land was plentiful, one-third of the Anglo households did not farm their own lands.

Unlike England, colonial America lacked major cities, as nine in ten colonists lived in communities less than 2000. By mid-century, however, developing American urban centers – Philadelphia, New York, Boston, Charles Town, Newport – were attracting budding populations.

With the burgeoning new wealth of the cities came filth, disease, crime and class tensions. In the larger cities, the wealthiest ten percent owned sixty percent of the taxable wealth, while the poorest sixty percent owned only ten percent of the wealth. Although New England was renowned for its long life expectancies, within Boston itself, death rates approximated those in old England. But along with these urban problems also came printers, newspapers, libraries, taverns, and coffeehouses – mediums that could circulate new ideas and debate issues relevant to a population growing more diverse every day.

THE BIG EVENT
A BREWING CULTURAL WAR:
ENLIGHTENMENT & AWAKENINGS

The century after Columbus is remembered as the century of the Spanish conquest of America. The following century, at least among the English, can be remembered as a century of North American colonization. The third century after Columbus – the century before the ratification of the United States Bill of Rights – can be remembered as a century of world wars and slave exchanges. Indeed, at no other time in human history were so many Africans captured and transported in chains to serve as perpetual slaves in the New World. This century before the creation of the United States Constitution, however, has also been given by historians a more endearing title, "The Age of Enlightenment."

Although the Enlightenment is difficult to define in both time and content, the term is associated with the late 17th and 18th century intellectual emphasis on reason and individualism rather than on dogma and tradition. Enlightened thinkers placed a fundamental faith in human progress and in the ability of humans to control their own futures. Distrusting dogma in all forms, it challenged some orthodox forms of Christianity, especially Christian notions that the natural world could be best understood by an exegesis of the Bible rather than through observation and reason. Some Enlightenment thinkers like Sir Isaac Newton, the "father" of modern physics and the discoverer of natural laws, insisted that the emerging science supported Christian faith. Other Enlightenment thinkers discarded Christian orthodoxy and became Deists, Christian Rationalists, or Latitudinarians.

Deists believed in a divine being who created the world, but rather than predestining events, left humans alone to work out their own destinies. According to Deists, God established natural moral laws that set boundaries between good and evil, but these laws had to be discovered by observing the natural world that God had created. Deists rejected atheism, and insisted that God could be known, but many were uninterested in church rituals and doctrines. To them, God was removed from human affairs. Like a clock maker who made a perfect clock that could run by itself without the need of further tinkering, God created a universe and set it in motion, but had no need to meddle with its inner workings. God did not send floods and fire as punishments for misconduct or rain blessings on the religiously active, or predestine some for salvation and others for damnation. Progress, if it was to be achieved, depended on human efforts to build institutions, promote learning, and live virtuous lives.

Akin to the Deists were Christian Rationalists, who also rejected the Puritans' focus on human sinfulness and the threat of severe divine punishments. For Christian Rationalists, God's greatest gift was the gift of reason, which if correctly followed, would lead all to the truths of Jesus' moral teachings.

Latitudinarians were Anglicans who aspired to emphasize the reasonableness of Christianity. A leading spokesperson who articulated latitudinarian principles was Archbishop John Tillotson. Stressing God's mercy rather than God's wrath, Tillotson understood the divine as a loving father who wanted to bestow eternal blessings on his children. Because of the centrality of this belief, Tillotson rejected the Calvinistic doctrine of predestination, stating:

> I am as certain that this doctrine [predestination] cannot be of God as I am sure that God is good and just, because this doctrine grates upon the notion that mankind have of goodness and justice. This is that which no man would do, and therefore cannot be believed of infinite Goodness. If an apostle, or an angel from heaven, teach any doctrine which plainly overthrows the goodness and justice of God, let him be accursed. For every man hath a greater assurance that God is good and just

than he can have of any subtle speculations about predestination and the decrees of God.

Not everyone in America or in Europe during this Age of Reason subscribed to these enlightened tenets. To many, this philosophy, and the liberal religions that often went with it, was dull, cold, and impersonal, if not outright blasphemous. Like the Puritans before them, those in this camp decried the spiritual apathy in many established churches, but unlike the Puritans, they encouraged individuals to trust their hearts and not their heads in spiritual matters. Insisting that God speaks to humans intuitively as well as intellectually, they yearned for a livelier form of spirituality that was centered on a joyous experience of the "New Birth."

In the middle decades of the 18th century, growing numbers in England (Methodists), Germany (Pietists), and France (Catholic Jansenists) turned to more inward and personal expressions of religious piety. The transnational and simultaneous appearances of more heartfelt forms of religion among Protestants and Catholics alike suggests that the Enlightened understanding of the universe as a machine and its creator as an impersonal force did not satisfy the psychological needs of everyone. The Enlightenment and its opposite, emotional religious outpourings, were two sides of the same coin. Some people were attracted and others repulsed by the efforts of Enlightened thinkers to throw off divine mysteries and the yoke of tradition and replace them with the freedom to use one's rational powers to make sense of the cosmos.

Even as Methodists in England and pietistic sects on the European continent were warming to more emotional forms of religion, in the British colonies a number of ministers began injecting greater emotion into their preaching, calling souls to become awakened to God by focusing more on eternal treasures than temperate riches. This brand of preaching resonated with large numbers of formerly spiritually apathetic parishioners. In the 1720s and 1730s, after decades of declining church participation, religion again became a focus in many local communities across the colonies.

Ripples of revival began to appear under the preaching of New Jersey's Dutch Reformed pastor Theodore Frelinghuysen, Pennsylvania's Presbyterian pastor Gilbert Tennent, and Massachusetts's Congregationalist pastor Jonathan Edwards. The colonies and denominations associated with these preachers demonstrate that the early awakenings were broad-based and not the work of a single sect or region. These local revivals would be galvanized into something even larger, a truly "Great Awakening," when the grand evangelist George Whitefield arrived from England.

AN ODD COUPLE MEET: BEN FRANKLIN & GEORGE WHITEFIELD IN PHILADELPHIA

If one were to select a single American to epitomize a man of the Enlightenment, no better selection could be found than Benjamin Franklin. A consummate man of action and public spirit, Franklin embodied the spirit of optimism, reason, and enterprise that gave definition to the era. If overly prideful and ambitious, Franklin also was a public servant who threw himself into many causes, achieving fame as a businessman, educator, scientist, writer, politician, and diplomat.

Franklin was born in Boston in 1706, the tenth son of English immigrants who were devout Puritans. Neither his parents' religion nor his father's candle and soap-making shop appealed to Franklin, and at age seventeen, he left Boston for Philadelphia, where he found employment as a printer. Within six years, he opened his own printing shop, and prospered so well in the trade that he was able to quit his business in his forties. Franklin retired, not to a life of leisure, but to multiple careers in public service. He experimented with electricity; produced several inventions; organized a reading club; created with others a library, university, and fire department; and devoted decades of his life to the cause of independence and the establishment of a new nation.

An avid reader and man of the world, Franklin had heard about George Whitefield before the Anglican minister arrived in Philadelphia. Although not irreligious, Franklin had no interest in Whitefield's obsession with being "born again." As Franklin wrote in his autobiography:

> Sunday being my studying day, I never was without some religious principles. I never doubted, for instance, the existence of the Deity; that He made the world, and governed it by His providence; that the most acceptable service to God was the doing good to man; that our souls are immortal; and that all crime will be punished, and virtue rewarded, either here or hereafter.

As a printer businessman, however, Franklin saw the coming of Whitefield as a grand opportunity to sell books and newspapers. Whitefield, after all, was the most popular celebrity to cross the Atlantic for America. Franklin attended Whitefield's first outdoor service and many subsequent ones because it was the talk of the town. Because Franklin was a curious man of science, he enjoyed observing people, and no event in his life attracted so many people to a single location as did the announced services of this preacher-entertainer.

After their first meeting in 1739, Franklin and Whitefield became both business associates (Franklin printed and sold Whitefield's Sermons and Journals) and friends for life. With Whitefield always concerned for Franklin's spiritual health, and Franklin for Whitefield's physical health, Franklin was Whitefield's best American friend and Whitefield was Franklin's only evangelical friend.

Despite their lasting friendship, they were an odd couple. Franklin was a jovial deist, Whitefield a sober Calvinist; Franklin, a charming womanizer with youthful vitality even as an aging man, Whitefield a strict Methodist who sought warmth from above, not from human hands, even as a youth; Franklin an American born businessman, scientist, and politician; Whitefield an English born Anglican minister and evangelist.

Their worlds and missions were different, but even with these great differences, they shared more in common than most of their contemporaries realized. Both were men with large egos who enjoyed being the center of attention. Both were self-made men who were beloved far from home. Both achieved their international fame by learning to exploit the emerging new technologies of their age – the postal service, newspapers, and transatlantic travel. Both had little interest promoting any particular religious sect and instead felt that disputes over religious doctrine were petty and unedifying, but built their careers around a distrust for hierarchical institutions. For Franklin, this was the British Crown; for Whitefield, the Church of England. Both left memoirs designed to teach the young how to find happiness, Franklin focusing on temporal and Whitefield on eternal happiness. The life work of both questioned the wisdom of placing unbridled trust in human sources of authority. Both died as American heroes.

Americans loved Franklin because he personified those things Americans held most dear: self-discipline, hard work, ambition, rationality, optimism, and voluntarism. America's love affair with Whitefield was more surprising because of his birthplace, religious asceticism, and Anglican ministerial status. Despite these things, Americans adored Whitefield because he was a splendid showman at a time most Americans were unacquainted with theater, and he was an outspoken "tell it like it is" critic of the social and religious hierarchies that growing numbers of Americans found distasteful.

Whitefield boldly followed the dictates of his conscience and had no qualms about (and even appeared to enjoy) defying social norms. Whereas most ministers aspired to be scholar-preachers who defended the doctrines of their particular denomination, Whitefield aspired to be an actor-preacher who spoke in the name of no denomination and whose mission was to enliven the faith, not define it. As one Anglican minister wrote in disgust, "to the Quaker, [Whitefield] becomes a Quaker; to the Anabaptist an Anabaptist; to the Presbyterian and Independent, a Presbyterian and Independent."

When Whitefield's superiors within the Church of England tried to corral his message, he publicly rebuked them, suggesting that many were yet unconverted. He published in his journals similar comments about New England's Puritan pastors, stating, "Many, nay most that preach, I fear do not experimentally know Christ." When these indiscretions caused him to be barred from Anglican pulpits, Whitefield bolted the church house for the out-of-doors, preaching to larger assemblies than had ever gathered together on American soil.

When further threatened with ministerial censure and suspension, Whitefield again took to the offensive, asserting that he would regard such a suspension "as much as I would a Pope's bull." Armed with publicists and printer friends like Franklin, Whitefield used the press to his advantage, securing for himself a martyr's image, and for his foes, an image of unregenerate tyrants. Portrayed as a David taking on Goliath, Whitefield became America's first mass entertainer and hero. A marketing marvel, Whitefield demonstrated that at least certain brands of religion could flourish without the support of established religious and state authorities.

THE AFTERGLOW: RELIGIOUS AFFAIRS AFTER WHITEFIELD

After visiting most of the colonies, Whitefield departed for England in December 1740, but he never forgot America, returning to his second home on seven occasions during his preaching career. By the time of his death in 1770, Whitefield had preached some 18,000 sermons to hundreds of thousands of listeners around the world. No other colonial era preacher received such notoriety, but many tried to follow in his footsteps, becoming traveling evangelists rather than settled ministers. Although few could equal his oratory skills, many emulated his dramatic methods, incorporating passionate gesturing, weeping, singing, and shouting into their messages. In his wake, extemporaneous delivery became more common, and ministers who continued to read their sermons did so self-consciously or apologetically.

Not everyone supported the message and methods of the revivalists. Conservative and moderate clerics expressed disgust with the "fanaticism" that accompanied many revivals. Some opposed the practice of sending uninvited traveling ministers into areas already served by other churches, and even more took offense at their accusations that many local pastors were unregenerate. Still others rejected as unbiblical the willingness of the revivalists to allow white women and African Americans to exhort in religious services.

Rationalists like Franklin were more amused than bewildered by the infighting taking place among the polarized Christian denominations. Franklin never warmed to Whitefield's brand of faith, but neither did he forget his friendship. Shortly before Whitefield's death, Franklin remarked, "He is a good man and I love him."

Franklin was not the only American to express these sentiments, for upon Whitefield's death he was mourned like no other man until the death of George Washington. Whitefield's refusal to stand firm against the institution of slavery prevented him from becoming one of the heroes of African American history, but upon his death, at a time when many white Christians still questioned whether African slaves had souls, Whitefield was known as one of the American slaves' best friends. The still seventeen-year-old African American poet Phyllis Wheatley mourned the loss of Whitefield with these words:

> Hail happy saint on thy immortal throne!
> To thee compliance of grievance unknown:
> We hear no more the music of thy tongue,

Thy wonted auditories cease to throng.
Thy lessons unequal'd accents flow'd!
While emulation in each bosom glow'd;
Thou didst, in strains of eloquence refin'd
Inflame the soul, and captivate the mind.
Unhappy we, the setting Sun deplore:
Which once was splendid, but now it shines no more;
He leaves the earth for Heaven's unmeasur'd height:
And worlds unknown, receive him from our sight;
There WHITEFIELD wings, with rapid course his way,
And sails to Zion, through vast seas of day.

POSTLUDE
IMMEDIATE CONSEQUENCES: SOCIETY & CULTURE AT MID-CENTURY

The Franklin/Whitefield friendship was unique, in part, because the two movements that their lives personified – the Enlightenment and the Awakening – were as incompatible as oil and water. Yet, ironically, these competing traditions shared some things. Both the Enlightenment and the Awakening brought into question the legitimacy of traditional sources of authority, encouraged individuals to pursue their own self-interests, and created an expectation of a future more glorious than the past.

The emphasis of the Great Awakening on personal spiritual experiences made converts less dependent on external authorities – scriptural or ecclesiastical. After the Awakening, it was possible to join another church or even hold services in the home rather than worship at a place that did not provide spiritual edification. The controversies provoked by the revivals convinced thousands that it was more important to obey one's conscience than to submit to the authority of ministers. Customs of courtesy and deference were not eliminated, but they were loosened as increasing numbers of common folk reached the potentially subversive conclusion that sometimes it was necessary to take matters into their own hands. As masses of newly awakened converts criticized their ministers for uninspiring worship, sometimes even accusing them of being unconverted themselves, disputes over ministerial spiritual authority arose that broke apart hundreds of churches. In New England, church separations weakened the church and state alliance as members of schismatic churches no longer supported public taxation for ministerial support.

The Great Awakening, thus, not only brought more people into churches, it also motivated individuals to move freely from one Christian denomination to another one that worshiped in ways more amenable to their individual tastes. The Christian denomination that grew most rapidly because of the Awakening was the Baptist sect. Before 1740, there were only sixty Baptist congregations in all of North America. During the next half century, the revival fires of the Awakening resulted in the establishment of nearly one thousand Baptist congregations, which appeared in virtually every English colony.

Presbyterian and Congregational churches also grew in numbers, although in the wake of the controversial revivals these denominations divided internally between the New Lights, who supported the new methods of evangelism, and the Old Lights, who held fast to the Calvinistic doctrine of predestination. Many colonists who were repelled by the excesses of the revivals associated with more moderate Anglican, Presbyterian, and Congregational churches, decided to associate with smaller sects like the Quakers, or attended no church at all. The heat of the revival also inflamed anti-Catholic passions, thereby giving Roman Catholics added incentives to turn inward among themselves.

The controversies of the awakening also encouraged greater missionary work and the establishment of additional colleges to train more colonial ministers. In 1754, New England ministers established as an evangelistic enterprise a New Light Indian School, which in time became incorporated as Dartmouth College. Converts from the northern colonies volunteered to become missionaries into the southern colonies. By mid-century, Presbyterian ministers from New York and New Jersey and Baptist preachers from New England were evangelizing in Virginia and the Carolinas. To train these and other ministers, the Presbyterians established Log College, which in time became known as Princeton University, and the Baptists erected a school that later received the name Brown University. About this same time King's College (later Columbia University) was founded largely to educate Anglican ministers and Queen's College (later Rutgers University) was incorporated largely to train Dutch Reformed ministers.

Interest in the colonial revivals and their ensuing controversies fused communication networks that linked Maine to Georgia, and the British colonies to evangelicals in England and Scotland. Before the 1740s, most newspapers in the colonies reported primarily European news. During the Great Awakening, however, colonial newspapers reported details of the traveling evangelists' preaching tours and detailed the controversies that followed their revivals. For the first time, colonists from Massachusetts were reading about events that were happening in Savannah, Charles Town, Philadelphia, and New York. In 1740 alone, colonial presses printed thirty-three Whitefield imprints, and eleven newspapers from Charles Town to Boston covered his revivals in detail, providing him advanced publicity for his meetings. Suddenly, there were new and growing lines of communication between the thirteen colonies, and colonists from south to north found pleasure in reading about a truly inter-colonial "American" phenomenon.

The egalitarian message of the evangelists also carried social consequences. The centrality of the idea that the new birth was open to all – men, women, rich, poor, master, servant – appealed to many slaves. During this revival season, for the first time African Americans accepted Christianity in large numbers. African participation at the gatherings both as attenders and exhorters often elicited press coverage both in the colonies and Britain, creating for some great concern, and for others an excitement that God was preparing the land for a coming new age.

Like the Deists and Christian Rationalists, most revival supporters and foes alike rejected the notion that there was a chain of authority that ran from God, to ruler, to people. Confident in the powers of human rationality, Enlightenment thinkers had long criticized the concept of divine right rule as antiquated and replaced it with another creed: coercive civil authority comes only from voluntary consent, and exists for the sole purpose of promoting the security, welfare, or happiness of the people. For centuries, most Christians had acknowledged God to be the source of government, but whether obedience was demanded to all rulers or only to moral rulers was an unresolved question. At mid-century, growing numbers of Christians were joining with the enlightened social philosophers in rejecting the idea of unqualified obedience, insisting that governments were created by consent and had to meet a moral test before they could claim legitimate coercive powers over the people.

By mid-century, most colonists of all religious stripes were accepting the premise that it was more important to obey one's conscience than to award unquestioned allegiance to any human power. The controversies surrounding the revivals also forced many commoners to reflect upon theories long pondered by the educated elites: what is the source of legitimate authority, and under what conditions is resistance to it morally justified?

ENDURING CONSEQUENCES: GIVING BIRTH TO THE AMERICAN MIND

During the middle decades of the 18th century, two grand events encouraged the English colonists living in America to consider themselves as Americans, or at least as American-English men and women. The first was the religious revitalization movement known as the Great

Awakening, which stirred debate and focused the attention of the colonists on events taking place on American soil. Contemporaneous with these awakenings was a second phenomenon that galvanized the colonies together. After a quarter century of peace, global conflicts between Britain and her perennial Catholic enemies, France and Spain, were resumed. In these mid-century world wars, the American colonists would become principal participants, not mere spectators.

Between 1739 and 1748, King George's War pitted the British against the Spanish, French, and Prussians. To help the motherland in this war, American colonists attacked and conquered Louisbourg, a French fortress in Nova Scotia. This campaign and victory was reported widely in colonial newspapers, as was the later disappointing and shocking news that the British government had returned the fort to the French in the treaty that ended the war.

This American victory and subsequent slight both bolstered colonial self-esteem and added to anti-British sentiments. It also contributed to the change in the hearts and minds of those living in North America. With a growing sense of pride and purpose, the colonists began to see themselves as a separate people. They were no longer simply English. They were becoming Americans.

Just a few years after the peace settlement ended King George's War, an incident in the colonies provoked yet another conflict between Britain and France. In 1754, Virginia sent a twenty-two-year-old Lieutenant Colonel named George Washington with two hundred militiamen to drive French settlers from Fort Duquesne, a trading post at the junction of the Allegheny and Monongahela Rivers (site of current day Pittsburgh). Washington failed at his mission to drive the French out of the Ohio River Valley, but his skirmish did provide a conflict between the British Americans and the French. Because the French also won the support of a number of North American Indians, this war in America became known as the French and Indian War.

In the summer of 1754, colonial representatives from a number of colonies, including Benjamin Franklin of Pennsylvania, met with Iroquois leaders in Albany, New York. The central objective of this Albany Congress was to persuade the Iroquois not to ally with the French. Franklin, however, used the occasion to propose the Albany Plan of Union, a plan for a council of representatives from each colony to ensure for a united defense. To Franklin's dismay, the delegates rejected his plan, but securing union among the colonies would remain dear to Franklin's heart for the remainder of his life.

Meanwhile, Britain sent two army divisions under General Edward Braddock to remove the French from the

Ohio River Valley. The arrogant British General disregarded the advice of colonial leaders by refusing to acknowledge the Native American peoples' claim to these western lands, thereupon alienating the Indians. With almost no support from native leaders, in 1755 the British were routed by their French and Indian adversaries, making it even more difficult to persuade future Native American peoples to bow to British authority.

After two years of fighting in America, in 1756 Prussia, an ally of Britain, invaded Austria, an ally of France. When France aided Austria and Britain assisted Prussia, the French and Indian War expanded into what in time would be called the Seven Years' War (1756-1763), another world war, which pitted the British against the French and Spanish empires. This fourth world war in less than a century differed from the earlier ones in that this war had American origins.

Great catastrophes often inspire speculations about the end of times, and this war was no exception. During the Seven Years' War, many colonists prayed that this war would end the enduring apocalyptic struggle between Protestants and Catholics. For many, the very scale of this war, which was fought from Calcutta to the Caribbean, signified the coming of the last days before Jesus Christ would return to inaugurate a millennial kingdom of peace.

The Protestant awakenings and the Anglo-French wars of the 1740s and 1750s fueled a virulent anti-Catholicism aptly captured by the words one chaplain sent to his troops: "Antichrist must fall before the end comes..... The French now adhere and belong to Antichrist, wherefore it is to be hoped, that when Antichrist falls, they shall fall with him." Like this chaplain-soldier, many colonists associated the Protestant tradition with spiritual and political liberty, and Catholicism with tyranny and the "infernal horrors of Popery." By the end of the Seven Years' War, "popery" stood as a synonym not only for Catholicism, but for any form of oppression.

During the early years of this bloody conflict, the British suffered military setbacks across the globe, including in America where colonists, still fuming at Britain for returning Fortress Louisbourg to France at the end of the last world conflict, did little to assist the British armies. The tide of the war turned when the veteran English politician William Pitt came out of retirement to direct the war effort. His strategy of sending massive funds but not armies to the Prussians; of launching all out assaults against the French in India, Africa, and the Caribbean; of treating the colonial militias as equal partners; and of promising the colonists that they would not be expected to bear the costs of the war, made him popular in America. With strong colonial assistance,

British fortunes returned, and by 1763, the British adversaries were ready to negotiate a peace settlement.

For many Protestant colonists, the peace settlement reaffirmed their conviction that God was on their side. In the Treaty of Paris, France surrendered New France (Quebec) and Spain lost Florida to the British. France also ceded to Spain its territories to the west. Consequently, after 1763 the map of North America was simpler than before the war, with Britain controlling territory from Florida to Canada east of the Mississippi River and Spain controlling the region beyond the Mississippi River. Although French settlers still lived in Canada and were promised the right to retain their Roman Catholic faith, after 1763 France no longer retained title to its North American empire. With the peace settlement, the American colonists anticipated an end to war-time taxes, unfettered access to lands to the west, and greater respect from British authorities across the Atlantic.

Unfortunately, these great expectations would not be realized, as the British victory came with a price: a massive war debt that Britain would need to be repay, and a treaty-required promise to protect Roman Catholicism in the New World. In response to this financial crisis, the British government expected the Americans to shoulder some of the financial burdens caused by a war they started. To the British, these expectations seemed entirely reasonable. To the

Americans, however, Britain's efforts to impose additional taxes and restrict the colonists' economic freedoms, as well as its promise to protect Roman Catholicism in Canada, would be viewed as encroachments against the basic liberties granted to all British subjects, no matter where they lived.

After the Peace of 1763, American resentment toward British colonial policies would grow along with a yearning hope for the dawning of a new millennial age. Contained within this rising American identity would be the seeds of a future rebellion.

PROBING THE SOURCES: The Awakening Among Friends & Foes

While most contemporaries acknowledged the presence of religious turbulence during the middle decades of the 18th century, discussions regarding the causes and the desirability of these developments varied widely. Presented below are excerpts from the writings of three influential authors who observed or participated in these events.

The first excerpt is from *The Memoirs of Benjamin Franklin*, later republished as the well-known *Autobiography of Benjamin Franklin*. This work was written in 1771 and 1784 by an older Franklin looking backwards to his youth. In these passages, Franklin recalls his observations of the revival and his relationship with George Whitefield. Why do you think Franklin included these accounts in his autobiography? How credible do you consider his descriptions to be?

The second piece is from Gilbert Tennent's *Danger of an Unconverted Minister*, a sermon that was delivered and printed in 1740. In this famous and controversial message, Tennent justifies sending evangelical Presbyterian ministers into areas already being served by Old Light Presbyterian pastors. Why do you think this publication provoked such controversy?

The final piece is an excerpt from *Enthusiasm Described and Caution'd Against,* a sermon published by Charles Chauncy in 1742. Charles Chauncy was a liberal minister of the First Congregational Church in Boston, and a leading opponent of the revivals. What would have motivated Chauncy to publish this warning?

Document 1: Excerpts from *The Memoirs of Benjamin Franklin* (1784). This work is available online at http://www.ushistory.org/franklin/autobiography.

In 1739 arrived among us from Ireland the Reverend Mr. Whitefield, who had made himself remarkable there as an itinerant preacher. He was at first permitted to preach in some of our churches; but the clergy, taking a dislike to him, soon refus'd him their pulpits, and he was oblig'd to preach in the fields. The multitudes of all sects and denominations that attended his sermons were enormous, and it was matter of speculation to me, who was one of the number, to observe the extraordinary influence of his oratory on his hearers, and how much they admir'd and respected him, notwithstanding his common abuse of them, by assuring them they were naturally half beasts and half devils. It was wonderful to see the change soon made in the manners of our inhabitants. From being thoughtless or indifferent about religion, it seem'd as if all the world were growing religious, so that one could not walk thro' the town in an evening without hearing psalms sung in different families of every street.

And it being found inconvenient to assemble in the open air, subject to its inclemencies, the building of a house to meet in was no sooner propos'd, and persons appointed to receive contributions, but sufficient sums were soon receiv'd to procure the ground and erect the building, which was one hundred feet long and seventy broad, about the size of Westminster Hall; and the work was carried on with such spirit as to be finished in a much shorter time than could have been expected. Both house and ground were vested in trustees, expressly for the use of any preacher of any religious persuasion who might desire to say something to the people at Philadelphia; the design in building not being to accommodate any particular sect, but the inhabitants in general; so that even if the Mufti of Constantinople were to send a missionary to preach Mohammedanism to us, he would find a pulpit at his service.

Mr. Whitefield, in leaving us, went preaching all the way thro' the colonies to Georgia. The settlement of that province had lately been begun, but, instead of being made with hardy, industrious husbandmen, accustomed to labour, the only people fit for such an enterprise, it was with families of broken shop-keepers and other insolvent debtors, many of indolent and idle habits, taken out of the jails, who, being set down in the woods, unqualified for clearing land, and unable to endure the hardships of a new settlement, perished in numbers, leaving many helpless children unprovided for. The sight of their miserable situation inspir'd the benevolent heart of Mr. Whitefield with the idea of building an Orphan House there, in which they might be supported and educated. Returning northward, he preach'd up this charity, and made large collections, for his eloquence had a wonderful power over the hearts and purses of his hearers, of which I myself was an instance.

I did not disapprove of the design, but, as Georgia was then destitute of materials and workmen, and it was proposed to send them from Philadelphia at a great expense, I thought it would have been better to have built the house here, and brought the children to it. This I advis'd; but he was resolute in his first project, rejected my counsel, and I therefore refus'd to contribute. I happened soon after to attend one of his sermons, in the course of which I perceived he intended to finish with a collection, and I silently resolved he should get nothing from me. I had in my pocket a handful of copper money, three or four silver dollars, and five pistoles in gold. As he proceeded I began to soften, and concluded to give the coppers. Another stroke of his oratory made me asham'd of that, and determin'd me to give the silver; and he finish'd so admirably, that I empty'd my pocket wholly into the collector's dish, gold and all. At this sermon there was also one of our club, who, being of my sentiments respecting the building in Georgia, and suspecting a collection might be intended, had, by precaution, emptied his pockets before he came from home. Towards the conclusion of the discourse, however, he felt a strong desire to give, and apply'd to a neighbour who stood near him, to borrow some money for the purpose. The application was unfortunately [made] to perhaps the only man in the company who had the firmness not to be affected by the preacher. His answer was, "At any other time, Friend Hopkinson, I would lend to thee freely; but not now, for thee seems to be out of thy right senses."

Some of Mr. Whitefield's enemies affected to suppose that he would apply these collections to his own private emolument; but I, who was intimately acquainted with him (being employed in printing his Sermons and Journals, etc.), never had the least suspicion of his integrity, but am to this day decidedly of opinion that he was in all his conduct a perfectly honest man; and methinks my testimony in his favour ought to have the more weight, as we had no religious connection. He us'd, indeed, sometimes to pray for my conversion, but never had the satisfaction of believing that his prayers were heard. Ours was a mere civil friendship, sincere on both sides, and lasted to his death.

The following instance will show something of the terms on which we stood. Upon one of his arrivals from England at Boston, he wrote to me that he should come soon to Philadelphia, but knew not where he could lodge when there, as he understood his old friend and host, Mr. Benezet was removed to Germantown. My answer was, "You know my house; if you can make shift with its scanty accommodations, you will be most heartily welcome." He reply'd, that if I made that kind offer for Christ's sake, I should not miss of a reward. And I returned, "Don't let me be mistaken; it was not for Christ's sake, but for your sake." One of our common acquaintance jocosely remark'd, that, knowing it to be the custom of the saints, when they received any favour, to shift the burden of the obligation from off their own shoulders, and place it in heaven, I had contriv'd to fix it on earth.

The last time I saw Mr. Whitefield was in London, when he consulted me about his Orphan House concern, and his purpose of appropriating it to the establishment of a college.

He had a loud and clear voice, and articulated his words and sentences so perfectly, that he might be heard and understood at a great distance, especially as his auditories, however numerous, observ'd the most exact silence. He preach'd one evening from the top of the Courthouse steps, which are in the middle of Market-street, and on the west side of Second-street, which crosses it at right angles. Both streets were fill'd with his hearers to a considerable distance. Being among the hindmost in Market-street, I had the curiosity to learn how far he could be heard, by retiring backwards down the street towards the river; and I found his voice distinct till I came near Front-street, when some noise in that street obscur'd it. Imagining then a semicircle, of which my distance should be the radius, and that it were fill'd with auditors, to each of whom I allow'd two square feet, I computed that he might well be heard by more than thirty thousand. This reconcil'd me to the newspaper accounts of his having preach'd to twenty-five thousand people in the fields, and to the ancient histories of generals haranguing whole armies, of which I had sometimes doubted.

By hearing him often, I came to distinguish easily between sermons newly compos'd, and those which he had often preach'd in the course of his travels. His delivery of the latter was so improv'd by frequent repetitions that every accent, every emphasis, every modulation of voice, was so perfectly well turn'd and well plac'd, that, without being interested in the subject, one could not help being pleas'd with the discourse;

a pleasure of much the same kind with that receiv'd from an excellent piece of musick. This is an advantage itinerant preachers have over those who are stationary, as the latter cannot well improve their delivery of a sermon by so many rehearsals.

His writing and printing from time to time gave great advantage to his enemies; unguarded expressions, and even erroneous opinions, delivered in preaching, might have been afterwards explain'd or qualifi'd by supposing others that might have accompani'd them, or they might have been deny'd; but *litera scripta Manet* ["the written letter abides"]. Critics attack'd his writings violently, and with so much appearance of reason as to diminish the number of his votaries and prevent their increase; so that I am of opinion if he had never written anything, he would have left behind him a much more numerous and important sect, and his reputation might in that case have been still growing, even after his death, as there being nothing of his writing on which to found a censure and give him a lower character, his proselytes would be left at liberty to feign for him as great a variety of excellences as their enthusiastic admiration might wish him to have possessed.

Document 2: Excerpts from Gilbert Tennent's *Danger of an Unconverted Minister* (1740)

And is it not the Command of God, that we should grow in Grace? 2 Pet. 3.18 and 1 Pet. 2.2. Now, does not every positive Command enjoin the Use of such Means, as have the directest Tendency to answer the End designed...? If there be a Variety of Means, is not the best to be chosen? else how can the Choice be called rational, and becoming an intelligent Creature? To chuse otherwise knowingly, is it not contrary to common Sense, as well as Religion, and daily confuted by the common Practice of all the rational Creation, about Things of far less Moment and Consequence?

That there is a Difference and Variety in Preachers Gifts and Graces, is undeniably evident, from the united Testimony of Scripture and Reason. ...

It is also an unquestionable Truth, that ordinarily GOD blesses most the best Gifts, for the Hearers Edification, as by the best Food he gives the best Nourishment. Otherwise the best Gifts would not be desireable, and GOD Almighty in the ordinary Course of his Providence, by not acting according to the Nature of Things, would be carrying on a Series of unnecessary Miracles; which to suppose, is unreasonable. The following Places of holy Scripture, confirm what hath been last observed. 1 Cor. 14. 12. 1 Tim. 4. 14, 15, 16. 2 Tim 1. 6 & Acts 11. 24.

If God's People have a Right to the Gifts of all God's Ministers, pray, why mayn't they use them, as they have Opportunity? And if they should go a few Miles farther than ordinary, to enjoy those, which they profit most by; who do they wrong?...

To bind Men to a particular Minister, against their Judgment and Inclinations, when they are more edified elsewhere, is carnal with a Witness; a cruel Oppression of tender Consciences....

Besides it is an unscriptural Infringment of Christian Liberty; 1 Cor. 3. 22. It's a Yoke worse than that of Rome itself....

Now, if it be lawful to withdraw from the Ministry of a pious Man in the Case aforesaid; how much more, from the Ministry of a natural Man? Surely, it is both lawful and expedient....

To trust the Care of our Souls to those who have little or no Care for their own, to those who are both unskillful and unfaithful, is contrary to the common Practice of considerate Mankind, relating to the Affairs of their Bodies and Estates; and would signify, that we set light by our Souls, and did not care what became of them. For if the Blind lead the Blind, will they not both fall into the Ditch?

Document 3: Excerpts from Charles Chauncy, *Enthusiasm Described and Caution'd Against* (1742)

[T]he Enthusiast is one, who has a conceit of himself as a person favoured with the extraordinary presence of the Deity. He mistakes the workings of his own passions for divine communications, and fancies himself immediately inspired by the SPIRIT of GOD, when all the while, he is under no other influence than that of an over-heated imagination. ...

But in nothing does the enthusiasm of these persons discover it self more, than in the disregard they express to the Dictates of reason. They are above the force of argument, beyond conviction from a calm and sober address to their understandings. As for them, they are distinguish'd persons; GOD himself speaks inwardly and immediately to their souls.... They feel the hand of GOD moving them within, and the impulses of his SPIRIT; and cannot be mistaken in what they feel.... And in vain will you endeavor to convince such persons of any mistakes they are fallen into....

Now, whoever, under the pretence of being guided by the spirit, set up one minister in opposition to another, glory in this minister to the throwing undue contempt on that, thereby obstructing his usefulness, and making way for strife and divisions, they are not really acted by the SPIRIT, whatever they may pretend....

Not that one minister may not be preferr'd to another; this is reasonable: But no minister ought to be regarded, as tho' he was the author of our faith; nor, let his gifts and graces be what they will, is he to be so esteemed, as that others must be neglected, or treated in an unbecoming manner....

And it deserves particular consideration,... the encouraging WOMEN, yea, GIRLS to speak in the assemblies for religious worship, is not a plain breach of that commandment of the LORD, wherein it is said, Let your WOMEN keep silence in the churches; for it is not permitted to them to speak....

The disorder of EXHORTING, and PRAYING, and SINGING, and LAUGHING, in the same house of worship, at one and the same time... [a]nd whatever the persons, guilty of such gross irregularity may imagine, and however they may plead their being under the influence of the SPIRIT, and mov'd by him, 'tis evidently a breach upon order and decency; yea, a direct violation of the commandment of GOD, written on purpose to prevent such disorders: And to pretend the direction of the SPIRIT in such a flagrant instance of extravagant conduct, is to reproach the blessed SPIRIT, who is not, as the apostle's phrase is, the author of confusion, but of peace, as in all the church of the saints.

There is, I doubt not, a great deal of real, substantial religion in the land. The SPIRIT of GOD has wro't effectually on the hearts of many, from one time to another: And I make no question he has done so of late, in more numerous instances, it may be, than usual. But this, notwithstanding, there is, without dispute, a spirit of enthusiasm, appearing in one place and other. There are those, who make great pretences to the SPIRIT, who are carried away with their imaginations: And some, it may be, take themselves to be immediately and wonderfully conducted by him; while they are led only by their own fancies.

WHAT OTHERS SAY: The Awakening & Its Consequences

For more than 170 years, historians have debated the significance of the colonial revivals of the mid-18th century. Below are three entries in this debate by three distinguished scholars. On what do these historians agree and disagree? How do you explain the differences in their interpretations?

Document 1: Excerpts from Jon Butler, *Awash in a Sea of Faith: Christianizing the American People* (Harvard University Press, 1990), pp. 164-65

Historians usually focus on the "Great Awakening" of the 1740s as the principal religious occurrence of prerevolutionary American society. Since its first elucidation in Joseph Tracy's *The Great Awakening*, which was published in 1841 to provide historical support for America's nineteenth-century revivals, its interpretative significance has multiplied a thousandfold. In the 1970s and 1980s, various historians have seen in it nothing less than the first unifying event of the colonial experience, the origins of the evangelical tradition, and a major source of revolutionary antiauthoritarian and republican rhetoric.

This emphasis on the "Great Awakening" may say more about subsequent times than about its own. The term was not contemporary, nor was it known to the historians of the revolutionary early national periods.... Although Tracy coined the term, he limited his history to New England and wrote only fleetingly about revivals elsewhere in the 1740s. Internal descriptive and analytical inconsistencies belie the event's importance and even its existence; it is difficult to date, for example, because revivals linked to it started in New England long before 1730 yet did not appear with force in Virginia until the 1760s. Its supporters questioned only certain kinds of authority, not authority itself, and they usually strengthened rather than weakened denominational and clerical institutions. It missed most colonies, and even in New England its long-term effects have been greatly exaggerated. On reflection, it might better be thought of as an interpretive fiction and as an

American equivalent of the Roman Empire's Donation of Constantine, the medieval forgery that the papacy used to justify its subsequent claims to political authority. More important, an obsessive concern with it distorts important historical subtleties and obscures other crucial realities of eighteenth-century American religious development.

Document 2: Excerpts from Thomas S. Kidd, *God of Liberty: A Religious History of the American Revolution* (Basic Books, 2010), pp. 21-22

The Great Awakening of the 1730s and 1740s was the most profound social upheaval in the history of colonial America. Shaking American Christianity to its core and revitalizing religious commitment even as it threatened colonial America's institutional churches, this first American revolution would herald the political revolution of 1776. The Great Awakening shattered the staid world of religious hierarchy, upending formal religious practice, which tended to be very hierarchical and clergy-centered, with church attendance often required by law and seating in church determined according to social status. The ministers who preached long, rhetorical, and theologically sophisticated sermons were challenged by new figures like Whitefield, the electrifying young preacher from England, who began dramatically changing people's expectations of what churchgoing meant. He took his controversial, emotional preaching style out of the church buildings (from which he was banned) and into the fields, where ... he directly told assembled throngs that they needed to be born again. In the colonies, Whitefield caused an unprecedented sensation, which was fueled by newspaper advertisements about his travels and by the widespread publication of his personal journals. He ... broached the possibility that some established ministers might not actually be born again, converted Christians. Their accusations unleashed a flood of popular criticism against ministers, who had previously wielded nearly unquestioned authority over their congregations.

The Great Awakening introduced common people to an exhilarating new world of spiritual possibilities. Never before had so many people had a chance to speak for themselves. Laypeople with no religious training often "exhorted" in the revival meetings.... Women, children, African Americans, Native Americans, and the poor – all were suddenly free to speak out.... Educated white men listened to these usually silent or silenced folk and concluded that they were filled with the Spirit.... A new era of spiritual democracy had begun.

Document 3: Excerpts from Frank Lambert, *Inventing the "Great Awakening"* (Princeton University Press, 1999), pp. 5-11

Since the 1840s when minister-historian Joseph Tracy first applied the term *The Great Awakening* to the colonial revivals, scholars have considered the awakenings as a single, grand movement.... Many viewed it as the biggest event in British North America before the War for Independence. Then in his 1982 revisionist article,... [Jon Butler] deemed unwarranted the assessment of the Awakening as "the greatest event in the history of religion in eighteenth-century America...."

The facts from which revival promoters constructed the Great Awakening were, to them, "really real" and utterly convincing. First, they cited the huge crowds attending revival services.... They reported crowds of at least 1,000 on more than sixty occasions, including estimates of 20,000 gathered to hear George Whitefield preach in Boston and Philadelphia. Second, revival pastors attested to genuine conversion experiences.... Upon close questioning of the converts, ministers certified that their experiences were authentic and conformed to scriptural standards.

Critics, however, demurred, giving no credence to promoters' "facts."...

Opponents ... considered the revival to be an invention.... They charged revival promoters with, at best, gross exaggeration ... in their published accounts of events, and, at worst, with lies and deceits aimed at discrediting nonrevivalist ministers and currying popular favor....

The Great Awakening, then, is also about contestation, a sustained, intensive struggle over meaning that may be termed an early American cultural war. The exchange reflected the colonies' great social and ethnic diversity and religious pluralism as the revival exacerbated deep divisions and sparked acrimonious debate....

When criticizing each other, revivalists and antirevivalists alike demanded that their opponents adhere to standards of evidence insisted on by seventeenth-century Enlightenment thinkers.... Yet, while each regarded their critics' claims as matters of evidence, revivalists and antirevivalists alike elevated their own views to the status of unassailable matters of faith.

LOOKING BACKWARD/LOOKING FORWARD: Assigning Cause & Assessing Effect

A "Reconciling Points of View" Exercise:

Review the three primary sources in the "Probing the Sources" section and the three secondary sources in the "What

Others Say" section. For each set of sources, create a short list of areas in which the authors agree and disagree. In 500 words or less, write an essay in which you address one or both of the following questions: (a) How can these conflicting testimonies be explained and/or reconciled?; (b) How can these diverting historical assessments of the significance of the Great Awakening be explained and/or reconciled?

A Project Based Learning Assignment: Assessing Cause, Effect, and Significance

This chapter, which focuses on an amorphous phenomenon labeled by historians as "The Great Awakening," opens with some probing questions that challenge students to understand the causes and to assess the significance of this phenomenon. Gather with a group of students who have completed the "Reconciling Points of View" exercise and let each student share his/her conclusions. As a team, prepare a lecture (or write an article) in which you define and describe this 18th century religious revitalization movement, explain why it took place where and when it did, and discuss its significance. Share your project with your classmates.

SUGGESTED READINGS

The best biographies of George Whitefield are Harry Stout, *The Divine Dramatist: George Whitefield and the Rise of Modern Evangelicalism* (Eerdmans Publishing Company, 1991), Frank Lambert, *"Pedlar in Divinity": George Whitefield and the Transatlantic Revivals, 1737-1770* (Princeton University Press, 2002), and Jerome Dean Mahaffey, *The Accidental Revolutionary: George Whitefield and the Creation of America* (Baylor University Press, 2011). Also of interest is Peter Charles Hoffer, *When Benjamin Franklin Met the Reverend Whitefield: Enlightenment, Revival, and the Power of the Printed Word* (Johns Hopkins University Press, 2011).

For an introduction to Franklin, see Walter Isaacson, *Benjamin Franklin: An American Life* (Simon & Schuster, 2003), as well as the always readable *The Autobiography of Benjamin Franklin* (Dover Publications, 1996). The best single volume synthesis of the Great Awakening is Thomas S. Kidd, *The Great Awakening: The Roots of Evangelical Christianity in Colonial America* (Yale University Press, 2007). A classic, yet still useful introduction to the Enlightenment is Henry May, *The Enlightenment in America* (Oxford University Press, 1976). For an excellent general overview of religion in colonial America, see Patricia Bonomi, *Under the Cope of Heaven: Religion, Society, and Politics in Colonial America* (Oxford University Press, 2003).

ONLINE RESOURCES

Historical Drawings
Philip Lea's Pictorial Map of North America, 1685
http://www.loc.gov/resource/g3300.mf000041/

M. Burgher's Pictorial Map of North America, 1722
http://www.loc.gov/resource/g3300.mf000041/

Lewis Evans's Pictorial Map of the Middle Colonies, 1749
http://www.loc.gov/resource/g3790.ct000062/

Illustrations
Portrait of George Whitefield
http://digitalpuritan.net/wp-content/uploads/2013/09/George-Whitefield.jpg

Portrait of Benjamin Franklin
http://en.wikipedia.org/wiki/Benjamin_Franklin#mediaviewer/File:BenFranklinDuplessis.jpg

Maps
Shifting Patterns of Colonial Governments, 1682-1730
http://etc.usf.edu/maps/pages/2400/2437/2437.htm

Henry Popple's North American Atlas, 1733
http://www.loc.gov/resource/g3300m.gct00061/#seq-2

Colonial America During the French and Indian War, 1754-1763
http://etc.usf.edu/maps/pages/7700/7701/7701.htm

The Americas in 1763
http://www.loc.gov/resource/g3300.ar002201/

Quantitative Data

Colonial and Pre-federal Statistics – Z Series
http://www2.census.gov/prod2/statcomp/documents/CT1970p2-13.pdf

American Colonial Incomes, 1650 - 1774
http://www.nber.org/papers/w19861

INDEX

Abraham (Abram), 42-43
Act of Toleration, Maryland, 149
Adam and Eve, 17, 63
Adams, Herbert Baxter, 104, 108-112
Adams, John, 37
Africa, 80-83, 93, 143, 219, 247
Africans, 92, 143, 144, 150, 219, 223, 224, 226
Age of Enlightenment, (or Age of Reason), 226-230, 238, 242
Alaska, 59
Albany Congress, 245
Albany Plan of Union, 245
Alexander VI, 89
Alexander VII, 95
Algonquin, 138, 144-147, 160
American Revolution, 203
Anabaptists, 235
Ancestral Puebloans, 66
Andros, Sir Edmund, 206, 208
Anglicans, 167, 180, 207, 208, 209, 213, 228, 233, 234, 240
Anne, Queen of England, 207, 210
anti-Catholicism, 247
anti-Leisler factions, 208
antinomianism, 170
Arbella, 181
Arctic Circle, 68

Arizona, 66
Arnold, John H., 50
Arthur, Prince of Wales, 129
Asia, 55, 59-63, 81, 110
Asians, 60, 62
Austria, 246
authenticity of sources, 26
Aztec, 66, 90
Bacon, Nathaniel, 150
Balboa, Vasco de, 89
Baptists, 167, 240, 241
Barbados, 178, 218
Barry, John M., 193-194, 196
Belgium, 77
Berengia, 61, 63
Bering Strait, 59
Berkeley, Sir John, 179
Berkeley, William, 150
Beza, Theodore, 186
Bible, 17, 18, 19, 21, 41, 43, 126, 127, 151, 152, 155, 160, 165, 266
Bill of Rights, 226
Black Death, 74-75
Black Sea, 73
Bloch, Marc, 49
Boleyn, Anne, 130-131
Bonomi, Patricia, 273
Book of Common Prayer, 131, 176
Boston, 122, 123, 159, 161, 202, 207, 212, 213, 225, 231, 250, 255, 270
Bristol, 142, 201

278 INDEX

Britain, 37, 102, 209-212, 223, 242, 244-249
British, 211, 244, 248
Brown University, 241
Brown, Kathleen, 197
Burgher, M., 274
Burke, Edmund, 47
Burn, A.F., 44
Bushman, Claudia, 116
Bushman, Richard, 216
Butler, Jon, 265-267
Cabot, John, 124-125
Cabral, Pedro, 111
Cahokia, 68
Calcutta, 246
California, 68, 112
Calvert, Cecilius, 148
Calvert, George, 148
Calvin, John, 127, 151, 186
Calvinism, 151, 152, 157
Calvinists, 167
Cambridge, England, 162
Canada, 125, 248, 249
Canary Islands, 110
Cape Cod, 153
Cape of Good Hope, 83
Cape of Storms, 83
Cape Verde Islands, 89
Caribbean, 218, 219, 246, 247
Carlyle, Thomas, 47, 112
Carolinas, 178, 217, 220, 241
Carr, E.H., 49

Carteret. Sir George, 179
Cartier, Jacque, 125
Cathay (China), 57, 134
Catherine of Aragon, 129, 130, 146
Catholics, 128, 133, 148-149, 167, 176, 180, 207, 209-210, 224, 229, 240, 246
Cavaliers, 175
Central America, 64, 95
Chaco Canyon, 66
Chagas disease, 93
Charles I, 146, 148, 155-157, 176, 204, 207
Charles II, 176-181, 195, 204-207, 212, 218
Charles Town (Charleston), 178, 219, 225, 241
Chauncy, Charles, 250, 261-264
Chesapeake, 147, 148, 150, 206, 217, 220, 222, 223
Chile, 60
China, 63, 76, 125
Christian Rationalists, 227-228, 242
Church of England, 130-132, 151-153, 157-158, 163, 175-176, 192, 207, 209, 235
Cipango (Japan), 57
Civil War, US, 36, 37
Clio, 34
Cohen, Charles, 197
Coke, Sir Edward, 162-163
Colorado, 66, 69

Columbia University, 241
Columbian Exchange, 94-95
Columbus, Christopher, 37, 61, 70, 71, 79, 97-99, 102, 123-124, 226
Columbus, Christopher, historians on, 102-111
Columbus, Christopher, plan, 55-56, 79-80
Columbus, Christopher, voyages, 86-87, 119
Columbus, Ferdinand, 84
Comte, August, 48
Congregationalists, 230, 240
Connecticut, 162, 171, 172, 177, 216
Constantine, 31
Constantinople, 71
Cooper, Sir Anthony Ashley, 177-178
Cortés, Hernando, 90-91
Cotton, John, 161, 186
Cramner, Thomas, 132
credibility of sources, 26-27
Croatoan Island, 136
Cromwell, Oliver, 176, 205
Cromwell, Richard, 176
Crosby, Alfred Jr., 117
Crusades, 76
Cuba, 86
Dale, Thomas, 139
Dare, Virginia, 135
Dartmouth College, 240, 241

De La War, Lord, 139
Declaration of Indulgence, 207
Defender of the Faith, 129, 130
Deists, 201, 227, 233, 242
Delaney, Carol, 116
Diamond, Jared, 117
Dias, Bartolomeu, 81-82
Discovery, 137
divine right rule, 163
Dominica, 87
Dominion of New England, 206
Dutch Reform, 178, 230, 241
Dutch, 177, 178, 206, 217
Eastern Woodlands, 67
Edict of Nantes, 223
Edward VI, King of England, 131-132, 134-135
Edwards, Jonathan, 230
Eliot, John, 160
Elizabeth I, Queen of England, 130, 132, 134, 136, 137, 151
England, 32, 63, 122, 124, 148, 151, 155, 156-158, 176, 177, 180, 203, 210, 217, 220, 229, 230, 236, 241, 255
English Civil War, 175, 176
English Reformation, 129-135
enthusiasm, 170
Ericson, Leif, 70
ethics, 33-35
Europe, 55, 62, 63, 70, 71, 73, 74, 76, 77, 79, 81, 83, 89, 95, 103, 113, 124, 128, 133, 229

Evans, Lewis, 274
Ezra, 28
Ferdinand II, King of Spain, 57, 81, 96-99, 118, 129, 146
First Ecumenical Council, 31
Florida, 95, 125, 133, 177, 210, 219, 248
Fort Sumter, 37
Four Corners Region, 66
France, 77, 78, 81, 124, 125, 128, 155, 203, 205, 207-210, 229, 244-246
Franklin, Benjamin, 201, 231-238, 245, 249-259, 273, 274
Franklin, Benjamin, memoirs, 249-259
Franklin, John Hope, 49
Frelinghuysen, Theodore, 230
French and Indian War, 203, 245, 246, 275
French Revolution, 204
French, 116, 127, 133, 178, 210, 222-224, 244-248
Frobisher, Martin, 134
Fundamental Orders of Connecticut, 162
Gates, Thomas, 139
Gaustad, Edwin, 197
Genesis, Book of. 17, 18, 41-43
Geneva, 128
Genoa, 79
George I, 210, 224

George II, 210, 211, 212, 224
Georgia, 202, 211, 217, 223, 241, 252-254
Germans, 127, 128, 178, 208, 210, 224
Germany, 128, 229
Gilbert, Humphrey, 134, 135
Gilderhus, Mark, 51
Glorious Revolution, 204, 209, 213, 218
Godspeed, 137
Granada, 84
Grand Canyon, 125
Great Awakening, 230, 238-240, 243-244
Great Awakening, historians on, 265-271
Great Basin, 69
Great Britain, 210
Great Colonial Hurricane, 121
Great Khan, 57
Great Lakes, 68
Great Pestilence (Black Death), 74
Great Plains, 69
Greek mythology, 18
Greek-Persian War, 20
Greeks, 19, 20
Greenland, 20
Gregorian (New Style) Calendar, 30, 31, 32
Gregory XIII, 30, 31
Grey, Lady Jane, 131, 132
Guanahani, 85
Gulf of Mexico, 68

Gustavson, Carl G., 50
Gutierrez, Diego, 117
Half-Way Covenant, 173
Halicarnassus, 43
Hall, Timothy, 197
Hanover, 210, 224
Harrisse, Henry, 111
Hartford, 162
headright system, 140, 141, 144, 148, 149
Hebrews, 17-19, 28, 42-43, 122
Henrietta Maria, 146, 148, 155, 204, 207
Henry VIII, 130-132, 136, 146, 195
Herodotus, 20, 21, 42-44, 51
Herodotus, *The Histories*, 43-44
Hispaniola, 87, 93
historiography, 22, 38, 45, 50, 51
Hoffer, Peter Charles, 273
Hohokam, 66
Hooker, Thomas, 161
Hopewell, 67
House of Burgesses, Virginia, 140, 143, 217
House of Delegates, Maryland, 149
Hudson Bay, 210
Huguenots, 133, 223
Humboldt, Alexander von, 111
Hume, Ivor, 197
Hutchinson, Anne, 169-170, 197

Iberian Peninsula, 84, 124
Ice Ages, 61, 69, 73
Iceland, 70
Incas, 64, 66, 90
India, 18, 247
Institutes of the Christian Faith, 128
Inuit (or Eskimo), 68
Ireland, 95, 128, 131, 133-135, 224, 250
Irish, 134, 224
Irving, Washington, 104-108
Isaacson, Walter, 273
Isabella I, 57, 83, 84, 96-99, 118, 129, 146
Italy, 128
Jackson, Helen Hunt, 48
Jamaica, 48
James Edward Stuart, 207
James I, King of England, 137, 140, 147, 153, 155, 163
James II, King of England (also Duke of York), 178, 179, 204-208, 213
Jamestown, 116, 138-140, 147, 150, 154, 173
Jansenists, 229
Japan, 110
Jerusalem, 76
Jews, 84, 178
John II, King of Portugal, 80, 81, 83
Julian (Old Style) Calendar, 31, 32
Kidd, Thomas S., 267-269, 273

King George's War, 203, 244, 245
King Philip (or Metacomet), 172
King Philip's War, 172, 212
King Williams's War, 203, 209
King's College, 241
Labrador, 70
Lambert, Frank, 269-273
Las Casas, Bartolomé de, 96, 97, 111
Latitudinarians, 227, 228
Lea, Philip, 274
Leisler, Jacob, 208
Leo X, 127, 129
Leyden, Holland, 153
Lisbon, Portugal, 79
Liverpool, England, 142
Livy, 46
Locke, John, 178
Log College, 241
London Company of Virginia, 137, 138, 147, 198
London, England, 71, 142, 256
Lord Baltimore, 148, 149, 177, 209
Lot, 43
Louis XIV, King of France, 210, 223
Louis XV, King of France, 210
Louisbourg, Fortress, 244, 247
Louisiana, 210
Luther, Martin, 126, 127, 129
Lutherans, 128, 167, 178, 180

Machiavelli, Niccoló, 47
Madeira Islands, 79
Magellan, Ferdinand, 90
Mahaffey, Jerome Dean, 273
Maine, 125, 136, 240
manors, 71-72, 75-76
Marco Polo, 76
Markham, Clements R., 111
Mary I, Queen of England, 129, 131, 132, 146
Mary II, Queen of England, 207, 208, 209, 213
Maryland, 148-149, 177, 209
Massachusetts Bay Colony, 121-122, 155, 160-162, 167-171, 174, 177, 192, 213
Massachusetts, 209, 213, 230, 241
Massasoit, 154
Mather, Cotton, 214
Mather, Increase, 214
May, Henry, 273
Mayan Civilization, 65
Mayflower Compact, 154
Mayflower, 153
Means, Stephen, 40
Medieval Europe, 71-78, 118
mestizos, 92
Metacomet (also King Philip), 172
Methodists, 229, 230, 233
Mexica (Aztec), 66
Mexico, 63, 66, 90, 91, 93
Miller, Perry, 189-191

Minnesota, 68
Mississippi River, 67, 248
Mississippian Culture, 67-68
Missouri River, 67
Mogollon, 66
Mongolia, 59
Morgan, Edmund, 191-193, 196
Morrison, Samuel Elliott, 102, 116
mound builders, 67
Mount Olympus, 18
Muslims, 76, 83, 84, 95
Mystic, Connecticut, 171
myth, 24-25, 41-42
Napoleonic Wars, 204
Narragansett Bay, 167
Narragansett, 171
Navigation Acts, 205, 206
Netherlands, 124, 128, 177, 205, 208
Nevada, 69
New England, 151-175, 182-185, 202, 206-207, 212-217, 220-222
New France, 248
New Hampshire, 170-177, 206
New Jersey, 177, 179, 206, 230, 241
New Lights, 240
New Mexico, 66
New Netherlands (New York), 170, 177, 178
New York City, 202, 225, 240

New York, 170, 177-179, 202, 206, 208, 225, 241, 245
Newfoundland, 125, 210
Newport, Rhode Island, 225
Newton, Sir Isaac, 227
Newtown (Cambridge), 161
Niña, 55, 56, 99
Nine Years' War, 203
Ninety-five Theses, 126, 127
Nipmuck, 172
Nomandy, 112
Norsemen (or Vikings), 70, 71, 111
North Carolina, 125, 135
Northwest Passage, 125, 134
Nova Scotia, 210, 244
Oglethrope, James, 210, 211
Ohio Valley, 67, 245
Old Lights, 240, 250
Olmec, 65
Opechancanough, 147
oral history, 49, 50
Pacific Northwest, 68
Paris, France, 71
Parris, Reverend Samuel, 215
Payne, Francis, 144
Penn, William Jr., 179, 180
Penn, William Sr., 179
Pennsylvania, 177, 179, 180, 202, 216, 224, 230, 245
Pequot War, 171, 172
Pequots, 171

284   INDEX

Persians, 44
Peru, 60, 66, 91
Philadelphia, 201, 202, 225, 232, 241, 251, 253, 270
Phillip II, King of Spain, 131, 136, 146
Phoenicians, 44
Pilgrims, 152-155, 171, 173
Pint, 55, 56, 99
Pinzón, Martin Alonso, 99
Piombo, Sebastiano del, 118
Pitt, William, 247
Pittsburgh, 245
Pizarro, Francisco, 91
Plymouth Colony, 154, 155, 157, 171, 172, 198, 208
Plymouth Company, 137
Pocahontas, 146, 147
Ponce de Leon, Juan, 125
Popple, Henry, 275
Portsmouth, Rhode Island, 168
Portugal, 78, 79, 80, 81, 83, 89, 124, 128
Portuguese, 178, 217, 219, 220, 222
Powhatan, 138, 144-147
Presbyterians, 224, 230, 235, 240, 241
primary sources, 3, 15, 16, 21, 23, 25, 38, 44, 45, 51, 115, 271
Prince Henry the Navigator, 80, 112

Princeton University, 241
project-based learning, 22, 39, 50, 115, 116, 195,196, 272, 273
Protestant Reformation, 126-128
Providence, Rhode Island, 167, 168, 195, 196
Prussia, 246
Prussians, 244, 246, 247
Puerto Rico, 87, 125
Puritans, 133, 151-160, 164-165, 170, 172, 174, 175, 180, 182, 207, 212, 213, 227, 229, 231
Putnam, Ann, 215, 216
Quakers, 179-180, 235, 240
Quebec, 125, 248
Queen Anne's War, 203, 209
Queen's College, 241
Quetzalcoat, 90
Raliegh, Walter, 134, 222, 223
Ranke, Leopold von, 47
Reconstruction, US, 36
Restoration England, 176
Revolution of 1688 (or Glorious Revolution),204, 209, 213, 218
Rhode Island, 167, 168, 169, 170, 177
Rip Van Winkle, 104
Roanoke Island, 135, 136
Rolfe, John, 140, 143, 146, 147
Roman Catholic Church, 31, 76, 89, 126, 127, 133, 207, 240, 248, 249, 261
Rome, 71
Roundheads, 175

Royal African Company, 218, 219
Russia, 59, 61
Rutgers University, 241
Salem Witch Trials, 214-216
Salem, Massachusetts, 123, 163, 165, 166, 215
San Salvador, 37, 85, 100
Santa Maria, 55, 99
Sarai (Sarah), 43
Sarges, 112
Savannah, Georgia, 202, 241
Scandinavia, 70, 112, 128
science, 12, 18, 20, 21, 24, 25, 29, 48, 49, 110, 227, 232
Scotland, 210, 222
Scots-Irish, 224
Scottish, 224
Scrooby, England, 153
Sea Dogs, 134, 135, 137
secondary sources, 10, 38, 39, 46, 271
Selincour, Aubrey de, 44
Separatists, 152, 153, 154, 157
Seven Cities of Gold, 125
Seven Years' War, 203, 246, 247
Seymour, Jane, 131
Sicily, 73
Simmons, Franklin, 198
slavery, 28, 72, 84, 88, 101, 139, 143, 144, 149, 171, 178, 217-220, 222, 223, 226, 237, 242
Smith, John, 146, 198

Society of Friends (Quakers), 179-180, 235, 240
South America, 63, 64, 65, 90
South Carolina, 133, 211, 219, 220, 222, 223
Spain, 31, 57, 78, 81-91, 96, 124-129, 131, 133, 134, 136, 209, 244, 248
Spanish, 55, 61, 65, 66, 81, 84-93, 97, 97, 113, 116, 129, 133-138, 203, 209, 210, 219, 226, 244, 246
St. Augustine, Florida, 133
St. Lawrence River, 125, 134
St. Louis, 67
Stannard, David E., 104, 113-114
Stout, Harry, 197, 272
Susan Constant, 137
Swiss, 128, 224
Switzerland, 128
Taino, 85-87
Ten Commandments, 165
Tennett, Gilbert, 230, 259-261
Tenochtitlan, 66
Teotihuacan, 65
The Bloudy Tenet of Persecution, 182, 186-189
Tillotson, John, 228, 229
Tolles, Frederick, 216
Toscanelli, Paolo dal Pozzo, 79, 80
Tracy, Joseph, 265, 266, 269
Treaty of Paris of 1763, 248, 249
Treaty of Tordesillas, 89

Trevelyan, George Macaulay, 48
Triana, Rodrigo de, 56, 61
Utah, 66, 69
Verrazano, Giovanni da, 125
Vikings (or Norsemen), 70, 71, 79, 111
Virginia Company, 139, 147, 153
Virginia Gold, 140
Waldseemüller, Martin, 89, 117
Wales, 222
Wampanoags, 154, 167
War of Austrian Succession, 203
War of League of Augsburg, 209
War of Spanish Succession, 203, 209
Washington, Booker T., 8
Washington, George, 245
West Indies, 140
Wheatley, Phyllis, 237, 238
Whitefield, George, 201-203, 231-238, 241, 268, 270, 274
Whitefield, George, described by Franklin, 250-259
William III, King of England, 204, 208, 209, 213
Williams, Mary, 162
Williams, Roger, 121, 122, 162-168, 171, 181-189, 198
Williams, Roger, historians on, 189, 190-194
Wilson, Norman J., 50, 51

Winthrop, John, 121, 122, 157, 159, 161-165, 168, 169, 174, 175, 181, 182, 198, 213
Winthrop, John, historians on, 189, 191-192
Woolf, Virginia, 48
Wyoming, 69
Yamasee Indians, 219
Yamasee War, 219
Yáñez, Vicente, 99
Yersinia pestis, 73
Yucatan Peninsula, 65

www.ingramcontent.com/pod-product-compliance
Lightning Source LLC
Chambersburg PA
CBHW060945230426
43665CB00015B/2062